A Psychology of Grace

How grace heals our relationships and emotional pain

D0711022

Stuart K. Norris

Quotations of scripture text are from the Holy Bible, English Standard Version, copyright © 2001 by Crossway Bibles, a division of Good News Publishers. Used by permission.

Cover photo: Karen L. Norris

ISBN-13: 978-0615942810
ISBN-10: 0615942814

Contents

Prologue 5

Introduction: Grace & Self-Justification 7

1: Strategies of Self-Justification 11
Boasting, Judging, Denial, Rigidity, Legalism, Complicity,
Overbearing, Abdication, Letting go of Self-Justification

2: Living with Grace 55
Generosity, Compassion, Forgiveness, Respect, Love,
Gumption, Spirituality

3: Healing with Grace 107
Marriage and Family, Sexuality, Anger, Guilt,
Stress, Addiction, Depression

Conclusion: A Culture of Grace 153

Snapshots:
1: Strategies of Self-Justification 163
2: Living with Grace 167

Appendix:
Grace as the Key 169

Study Guide 175

Prologue

This is not an easy book to read. It isn't hard because it is hard to understand; it is hard because grace shows us things we'd rather not see, and dispenses with things we use to prop ourselves up.

Grace, on the other hand, can also show us a way of living that many of us hunger for. Although this book can be hard to read, it is only hard because we make it hard, and sometimes we are best able to find our way when we take the way that seems hardest.

In my work as a pastor, hospice chaplain, and licensed marriage and family therapist, I have seen the deep importance and healing presence of grace again and again. Grace helps us to see what we have been unable to see, make real changes, and find real connection with real human beings. It is hard to overestimate the importance of grace.

Introduction

Grace & Self-Justification

Suggest that someone is a liar, a wrongdoer, nasty, arrogant, selfish, a cheater, and see how they respond. Aside from fictional characters, no one really wants to think of themselves as bad or evil. If people do call themselves "bad" it is usually with tongue in cheek, while posturing, while trying to be intimidating, or while thumbing their noses at rules they consider illegitimate. None of us wants to think of ourselves as a bad person. And if we must admit that we have acted badly, we don't want to see ourselves as personally bad. We want to see ourselves as a good person, a person worthy of love and respect.

On the surface, this may seem like a benign or even a noble desire. But it can lead us to live a life of self-justification, a hurtful life in which we use various strategies to protect and promote our feeling of being a good person. We can embrace that life if we choose. Many of us do. Or we can do something different and choose grace. The focus of this book, therefore, is on grace and how choosing grace can lead to a very different life, a healing life in which we have no use for self-justification or any of the pain it brings.

A Psychology of Grace

Righteousness is not a word that we may commonly hear outside a church or religious service. It may even seem to have somewhat of an old-fashioned ring to it. But the word is just as important as it ever was, and not just in the context of religion. Righteousness refers to the quality of being good, of being true, of having real integrity. Righteousness is important, and we all know it. We may not normally use the word, or even think about it. But inasmuch as we want to see ourselves as a good person, and react to the suggestion that we are not, personal righteousness is not only important to us, it is a core concern.

Psychology is the study of why we do what we do, and our desire to see ourselves as a good person can account for much of why we do what we do. We can do what we do because we want to see ourselves as righteous, and have others see us as righteous. This perspective can put much of our emotional pain in a singular light. If it is due to our efforts to see ourselves as a good person (which can be the case more than we realize or care to admit), we can find healing when, through faith in the grace of God, we let go of self-justification.

In some schools of psychology, human motivations are understood as more or less determined by our biology, environment, or other factors beyond our control. But the choice between grace and self-justification is very much in our control. Grace is always a choice. There is never a reason that we can't choose grace. No matter how we were raised, no matter what our education, no matter what we have experienced, and no matter what our hereditary genetics, we can always choose grace. There may be times when we don't feel like choosing grace, but we always can; it is always a choice, and there is nothing that can stop us from making that choice. In the choice between grace and self-justification we have much to say about the quality and course of our lives.

A psychology of grace can be summarized in three points:

1. We suffer when we pursue self-justification.
2. We thrive when we choose grace.
3. We can always choose grace.

The Plan of This Book

In the following pages, I attempt to outline a psychology in which self-justification is seen as a major reason for psychopathology and grace as a key to healing. Chapter one, *Strategies of Self-Justification,* begins with the parable of the Tax Collector and the Pharisee, which illustrates self-justification. It then describes some common strategies we may use in our pursuit of self-justification. These are: *boasting, judging, denial, rigidity, legalism, complicity, overbearing* and *abdication.* The chapter concludes with seven reasons we may not let go of self-justification even though we profess faith in the grace of God.

The second chapter, *Living with Grace,* begins with the parable of the Good Samaritan which illustrates the grace we can extend toward one another. The grace of God not only encourages us to let go of self-justification, it shows us a way of living without self-justification. Just as God regards us with grace, we can regard one another with grace. We can think and act with grace; and as we do, we not only help one another, we help ourselves. This chapter looks at how we can choose to live with grace. It looks at *generosity, compassion, forgiveness, respect* and *love* as expressions of grace; and how *gumption* and *spirituality* are characteristics of a life of grace.

The third chapter, *Healing with Grace*, begins with a promise of healing Jesus made to those who follow him. He said: *Come to me, all who labor and are heavy laden, and I will give you rest. Take my yoke upon you, and learn from me, for I am gentle and lowly in heart, and you will find rest for your souls.* This chapter examines some of the psychological consequences of self-justification and how grace brings healing. Grace can bring healing to a troubled marriage and a dysfunctional family; it can bring sanity and beauty to sexuality; it can transform anger; and it can help us to find relief from guilt, stress, addiction and depression.

The conclusion, *A Culture of Grace*, looks at how grace can characterize a culture, such as the culture of a business, a classroom or a church; and how a church, when it is true to its calling, is an intentional culture of grace with the mission of defining grace, teaching grace, modeling grace, talking about grace, and encouraging the practice of grace in everyday life.

This book is entitled *A Psychology of Grace* because our choice between grace and self-justification has broad and profound consequences for our psychological well-being.

1

Strategies of Self-Justification

[Jesus] also told this parable to some who trusted in themselves that they were righteous, and treated others with contempt: "Two men went up into the temple to pray, one a Pharisee and the other a tax collector. The Pharisee, standing by himself, prayed thus: 'God, I thank you that I am not like other men, extortioners, unjust, adulterers, or even like this tax collector. I fast twice a week; I give tithes of all that I get.' But the tax collector, standing far off, would not even lift up his eyes to heaven, but beat his breast, saying, 'God, be merciful to me, a sinner!' I tell you, this man went down to his house justified, rather than the other. For everyone who exalts himself will be humbled, but the one who humbles himself will be exalted." (The Gospel of Luke, chapter 18, verses 9-14)

The Pharisee in this parable is an illustration of self-justification. He is trying to justify himself; he is trying to paint a picture of his life in which he stands as a good person, a person worthy of respect and applause. Self-justification is often thought of as something we may only do when we are trying to justify our particular words or actions. But inasmuch as we want to think of ourselves as a good person, self-justification is not merely about trying to justify our behavior; it is about trying to justify ourselves as a person. Note that the Pharisee isn't trying to defend himself because he was accused of doing something wrong; he is trying to justify himself as a person; he is trying to make a case for his personal righteousness. The Pharisee's goal was self-justification, and in his pursuit of that goal he made use of some specific strategies of self-justification. Like the Pharisee, we too can use strategies of self-justification. We may not be as obvious as the Pharisee, but we too can try to paint a picture of ourselves in which we stand righteous. We may then try to sell that picture, in whole or in part, to whoever is willing to buy it.

We may not want to think about strategies of self-justification unless we are thinking about how others are using them. But there are some important reasons why we should:

First, the more clearly we understand self-justification, the more clearly we can understand why we do what we do. We can see our self-justification. We can see how our self-justification influences our thoughts, guides our words, and determines our attitudes toward one another. We can see how it shapes our goals and values. It can be painful to think about self-justification and how we, like the Pharisee, may be trying to make a case for our righteousness; it may be the last thing we want to do. But it can show us a lot about ourselves.

Second, the more we understand self-justification, the more we can see how we sabotage ourselves. Self-justification can have all sorts of painful consequences; within us, in our relationships, and for those who follow us such as our children. If we don't understand self-justification, we may experience many of those consequences but have little idea of why they are happening or of how much we can do to prevent them from happening.

Third, the more clearly we understand self-justification, the more clearly we can see our choice: We can choose to let go of self-justification and live with faith in the grace of God, or we can choose to pursue self-justification. It is our choice, and the more clearly we see that choice, the more we can see that it *is* a choice.

An understanding of self-justification helps us to live with our eyes open. We can see where we are in our lives; we can see what we have been doing to put ourselves there; and we can see how we can go somewhere else if we choose. If it's our desire to live with faith in the grace of God, an understanding of self-justification can help us to see the meaning of that faith in some very real and practical terms. We'll begin by looking at some common strategies of self-justification: *boasting, judging, denial, rigidity, legalism, complicity, overbearing* and *abdication*. Then in the next two chapters, we'll look at how our choice between grace and these strategies can make a tremendous difference in our relationships and our emotional well-being.

Boasting

Boasting, as a strategy of self-justification, is an attempt to assert, prove, or otherwise display ourselves as personally righteous. In boasting, we don't just hope others will see us as a good person. We actively try to make and promote our case. We try to convince others to see us in a way we want them to see us. And when they do, that can help us to feel righteous. Boasting can also be a way of trying to convince ourselves of our righteousness.

Boasting can take a number of forms, such as:

- *Simple boasting*, in which we try to impress others with our righteousness.
- *Comparative boasting*, in which we try to prove ourselves better than others.
- *Imaginative boasting*, in which we imagine ourselves as righteous.
- *Hypocritical boasting*, in which we pretend to be more righteous than we are.

Simple Boasting

The Pharisee was making a simple boast when he said, *I fast twice a week; I give tithes of all that I get.* We can boast about all sorts of things. We may boast about our values, our diligence or thoughtfulness; our patience, wisdom or charity; our sacrifices or good deeds. We may even boast about our spirituality. One of the most common ways of boasting is to boast about things that seem to make us more respectable. We may boast about our power, beauty or physical strength; our maturity, intelligence, health or energy; our possessions, reputation, courage or charisma; our nationality, connections, social status, friends, awards or professional achievements. Any of these boasts may help us feel like a good person and possibly lead others to think of us as a good person.

Although we may normally think of boasting as an effort to point out strengths, we may also boast about our weaknesses. We may talk about our lack of money, poor health, awful job (or lack of one), etc. We may talk about our illnesses, symptoms, surgeries and medications. Any of these things can be used to make a case for our righteousness. Consider the following:

- We may boast of our poor health or lack of money in the hope that other people will admire our fortitude, patience, resourcefulness, perseverance, or faith in God.

- We may think of our suffering as balancing the scales against our past wrongdoings, and then advertise our suffering as a way of saying, "See how I have suffered? I have paid for my sins."

- Jesus said that those who follow him would suffer for their righteousness. So we may advertise our suffering as evidence of our righteousness. We may even wear our suffering like a war medal or a badge of honor.

- We may boast of our weaknesses to show how we are not responsible for our actions (and that we are therefore righteous in spite of our actions).

Comparative Boasting

In comparative boasting, we boast of our righteousness as compared with others. The Pharisee was making such a boast when he prayed, *God, I thank you that I am not like other men, extortioners, unjust, adulterers, or even like this tax collector.* He compared his life to that of people he saw as unrighteous, and felt an enhanced sense of personal righteousness in doing so. Although we may prefer to see ourselves as better than the Pharisee, we can do the same thing. For instance, upon seeing someone acting badly we may say something like, "I would never do that," "You would never see me in a situation like that," or "I can't imagine why anyone would do that." Although we are trying to hide behind wisdom and moral virtue, we are actually saying, "I'm better than that person, more righteous." We may also simply point out someone's bad or foolish behavior and leave our own comparative righteousness unstated.

In another form of comparative boasting, we compete with one another in a game of who is more righteous than whom. We can keep this competition to ourselves or we can declare it openly. When we do the latter we say something to the effect of:

"I'm right and you're wrong."
"I'm more conscientious than you are."
"I'm more responsible than you are."
"I work harder than you do."

In other words, "I'm more righteous than you are." Although each of those statements asserts some kind of moral superiority, comparative boasting is not limited to obviously moral issues. We can find an enhanced feeling of righteousness whenever we see ourselves as somehow superior. Although we may deny it as obviously false, there is an old fallacy that many of us nonetheless seem to believe in practice. It is known as the principle of *might makes right*. When we feel in some way mighty, we can also feel righteous.

It is as if we see any kind of superiority as evidence, if not proof, of our righteousness. This may not be rational, but that doesn't stop us from living that way. We may feel more righteous than others when we are faster, stronger, smarter, prettier, or luckier than they are. We may even feel more righteous than others when we get the best seat in a restaurant or win a board game.

Consider how this can work with sports. There are a number of reasons we may enjoy watching sports, but we may especially enjoy watching because it offers the possibility of winning an enhanced sense of righteousness whenever our team wins. Our sense of superiority and our boast of, "We won!" can be accompanied by an enhanced feeling of righteousness. The downside, of course, is that if our team loses, our sense of righteousness can seem to take a hit; but the hope of victory, and the feeling of righteousness that can accompany it, can keep us watching. In this light, we can see how watching sports can carry the same importance as a religion. It helps us feel righteous.

Imaginative Boasting

With imagination, we can create our own reality, a reality in which we are personally righteous. We can imagine ourselves as wise, kindhearted or generous. We can imagine ourselves as a good friend, perhaps the best friend anyone could ever have. In romantic fantasy, we can imagine ourselves admired and desired, the object of special attention. We can imagine a future in which we are a success in the eyes of the world. We can imagine everyone, including the kids we knew in school, finally seeing our true worth. We can even imagine ourselves standing vindicated in the eyes of God. All of these fantasies can enhance our feeling of righteousness.

If we win a prize on a lottery ticket, we can imagine ourselves as deserving it. To the question, "Why me when the chances were so slim?" our unspoken answer is, "I must be living right. God is smiling on me." In a casino, the exultant cry of, "I won!" may not only be about money. It may also be about winning God's imagined approval. In a more mundane example, if we walk into a post office expecting to see a long line, but find that there is no one before us, we can imagine God smiling upon us, rewarding us for our goodness. If we turn around after doing our business with the postal clerk and see that a long line has formed behind us, we may imagine ourselves as especially favored.

Imagination can help us in the competition over who is more righteous than whom. We can imagine virtues in ourselves and deficiencies in others that are actually not there. In our workplace, for instance, we can imagine people who work harder than we do as doing so for less than honorable reasons. We can imagine them as insecure, unsociable, incompetent, or trying to appear better than others. We can also imagine ourselves as the most important person in our workplace no matter how hard other people work.

Imaginative boasting is a powerful and versatile strategy of self-justification. The sky is the limit. If nothing else seems to be working for us, we can find a sense of personal righteousness in our own imagination. We can imagine ourselves as loved, famous and successful. And if we can't imagine that, we can at least imagine ourselves as misunderstood.

Hypocritical Boasting

Most of us are familiar with hypocrisy. It is putting on a false face, pretending to be someone we are not in the hope of impressing others. We put on a show like an actor on a stage. We play a part. If the part we play is convincing, other people may admire us, praise us and applaud us, helping us to feel righteous. We can even fool ourselves.

Jesus talked about examples of hypocrisy that were apparently common at the time. He said: *When you give to the needy, sound no trumpet before you, as the hypocrites do in the synagogues and in the streets, that they may be praised by others. ... And when you pray, you must not be like the hypocrites. For they love to stand and pray in the synagogues and at the street corners, that they may be seen by others* (Matthew 6:2-5).

Although we may not see such examples today, hypocrisy is as common as it ever was. We can pretend to be a hard worker when we're really not. We can pretend to care about people who are suffering when we really don't. We can pretend to be knowledgeable about a particular subject when we're actually not. We can put on a false face in all sorts of ways. One of the most popular kinds of hypocrisy, even so far as that it is often encouraged, is *bravado*. Bravado comes in many forms, some obvious, some well disguised. But in general, bravado is an attempt to put on a false face of confidence, wisdom and strength. We may actually be lost and insecure; but we try to portray ourselves as someone who knows who we are, knows what we are about, and knows the best way to conduct our lives.

Grace

There is no need to try to make a case for our personal righteousness. We can come before God just as we are (which is actually the only way we can come before God). In the parable of the Prodigal Son (Luke 15:11-32), the father welcomed his son without regard to what he had done. Although his son had prepared a speech, his father evidently didn't wait to hear it. He ran to him and hugged him and kissed him before he had a chance to say anything. He regarded his son with grace and received him with grace.

God regards us in the same way. No matter who we are, no matter how we think or feel about ourselves, no matter how other people think or feel about us, no matter what we have done and no matter how we have lived, God is there for us. There is nothing we can do to earn or deserve God's love. It isn't something we can bargain for. It is a gift, a pure gift.

Judging

Judge not, that you be not judged. For with the judgment you pronounce you will be judged, and with the measure you use it will be measured to you. Why do you see the speck that is in your brother's eye, but do not notice the log that is in your own eye? Or how can you say to your brother, 'Let me take the speck out of your eye,' when there is the log in your own eye? You hypocrite, first take the log out of your own eye, and then you will see clearly to take the speck out of your brother's eye.
(Matthew 7:1-5)

There is a lot of confusion about the meaning of *judging*. Some think it is always wrong to judge, and that we should never make any kind of judgment about another person; that we shouldn't make judgments, for instance, about anyone's behavior, honesty, or trustworthiness. But in this passage, Jesus doesn't condemn any kind of judgment. He condemns hypocritical judging, in which we focus on the faults of others while ignoring our own. Such judging is a common strategy of self-justification.

While Jesus spoke against hypocritical judging, he also taught about the importance of making other types of judgments. For instance, he said, *Beware of false prophets, who come to you in sheep's clothing but inwardly are ravenous wolves. You will recognize them by their fruits* (Matthew 7:15-16). And he taught the importance of judging rightly, saying, *Do not judge by appearances, but judge with right judgment* (John 7:24). Practically speaking, there are judgments we must make every day. We may need to ask:

"Can I trust what this person is saying?"

"Should I buy a car from this man?"

"Is this right or wrong?"

"Can this prospective employee do the job I need her to do?"

"Should I tell this person about my personal struggles?"

"Will my child use this gift responsibly?"

"Is the repairman doing a good job for me?"

"Should I allow this person to watch over my children?"

Clearly, these are all important judgments. We all need to make judgments about trust, morality, ability and quality; and we can do so without playing the Judge.

Jesus confronted hypocritical judging when he was presented with a woman caught in adultery. According to the law, the woman was to be stoned for her crime. When asked about the rightness or wrongness of this law, Jesus answered, *Let him who is without sin among you be the first to throw a stone at her* (John 8:7). He exposed their hypocrisy and the woman was spared. Jesus likewise says to each of us, *Why do you see the speck that is in your brother's eye, but do not notice the log that is in your own eye?* If we were to honestly answer that question, we would say, "Because it helps me to feel better about myself. It helps me feel righteous." If we want to see ourselves as a good person worthy of respect and approval, then focusing on the faults of others can help us do that.

It is worth noting that Jesus didn't refrain from making any kind of judgment about the woman caught in adultery. He made a very clear judgment about the morality of her adulterous behavior. After the crowd left, he said, *Woman, where are they? Has no one condemned you?* She said, *No one, Lord.* And Jesus said, *Neither do I condemn you; go, and from now on sin no more.* (John 8:10-11).

Hypocritical judging helps us feel better about our righteousness in at least two ways:

1. Focusing on the faults of others can help us feel better about ourselves in comparison. And the greater the faults, the more righteous we may feel. Playing the Judge is therefore famous for magnifying faults that are minor, imagining faults where there are none, and theorizing about faults that may be hidden. Like the Pharisee looking down on the tax collector, playing the Judge can help us feel righteous.

2. In playing the Judge we assume a lofty, self-righteous, godlike role in which we set ourselves up as a Judge of other people. We can then feel better about ourselves simply by virtue of our assumption of that role. Even if we judge others favorably, we can still feel an enhanced sense of our own righteousness because of the role we are assuming. Consider how this can be found in such fields as medicine, mental health, social work, education, religion and law enforcement, all of which require important judgments about people. If we are a member of one of those professions, we may not only use our position to make the judgments we need to make, we may use it to assume the lofty role of Judge and even find our greatest job satisfaction in the opportunities our work affords us to assume that role.

Judging, as a strategy of self-justification, can be spoken or unspoken. We can keep our judgments to ourselves or we can let them be known. When we choose the latter, we risk retaliation, censure and challenge, and we may regret our words; but we may also find a tremendous feeling of vindication in the pain we cause. We may walk away saying, "I sure got 'em with that one!" We may also attract others of like mind who support and encourage our judgments.

Unspoken judging, on the other hand, has different advantages. Although it may be more satisfying to pronounce our judgment, keeping it hidden can protect us from retaliation, censure, or the risk of having our judgment challenged. No one can interfere with our attempt to feel better about ourselves. Unspoken judging may not be as hidden as we think, however. Even when we are careful, our judging may still show in our look, gestures or body language.

Prejudice is a type of judging. With prejudice, we pre-judge someone on the basis of race, sex, age, nationality, education, religion, disability, class, etc. Prejudice is an easy strategy of self-justification. In ordinary judging, we may need to take some time to come up with a rationale for our judgment. But with prejudice, the rationale is already pro-vided and the verdict is already in. We don't need much evidence to support our prejudice and we can feel free to dismiss evidence that doesn't support it. (Although we may still find self-justifying satisfaction in evidence that does seem to support it.) We only need to identify someone as a member of a despised group. Prejudice can also provide an additional advantage for self-justification: with prejudice, we may not only see ourselves as better than one or a few individuals; we may see ourselves as better than millions.

Life is full of opportunities to play the Judge. We can judge our family members, our friends, our enemies and the people we see on television. We can judge our co-workers and the people we serve in our work. Wherever we see people we can play the Judge. We may not think of ourselves as the kind of person who plays the Judge. But inasmuch as we want to lift ourselves up or feel better than others, we may do so more than we realize; if not outwardly then in our own minds.

The grace of God leads us to let go of playing the Judge. With grace, there is no need for self-justification or any of the strategies that seem to support it. We can look at one another with clear, non-judgmental eyes; and if there are judgments we need to make, we can do so without playing the Judge.

Denial

Denial is a refusal to recognize or admit the truth. Although denial is often associated with alcoholism or the refusal to believe tragic news, we can be in denial about all sorts of things. We can be in denial about our health, the condition of our marriage, the consequences of our actions, the behavior of loved ones, and the quality of our work. We can be in denial about how we relate to others, how we think, and how we spend our time. There is no limit to the things we can be in denial about.

Denial, as a strategy of self-justification, is a refusal to believe anything that is not compatible with our preferred feeling of righteousness. If we want to see ourselves as a good person; if we want to believe that we relate to others with love and respect; if we want to believe that we are wise, fair and generous; if we want to think of ourselves as possessing respectable goals and values; we are motivated to deny anything that does not support those beliefs.

In denial, we deceive ourselves. If the truth doesn't support the way we want to see things, then we don't want to know the truth. We don't want to see it and we don't want to talk about it. We only want to see and hear what we want to see and hear. And we don't want to think about the ways in which we may be in denial. When we are invested in self-justification, we don't want to know the truth; we want to live in self-deception.

Some of the common strategies of denial include *rationalization, self-distraction, selective insight, laziness,* and *withdrawal:*

Rationalization

When we rationalize, we try to see ourselves, our circumstances and the people around us in ways that suit us. Rationalizations can be obvious and obtuse, or they can be sharp and sophisticated. They can be short or long, spoken or unspoken. They can have some truth in them or they can be altogether ridiculous. Whatever the case, a rationalization can be a way of saying "I'm righteous." Consider the following:

"I know I was mean, but she deserved it." (Therefore, I'm righteous.)

"Nobody's perfect." (Therefore, I'm righteous.)

"You have to live a little." (Therefore, I'm righteous.)

"It's no big deal." (Therefore, I'm righteous.)

"I know it wasn't ethical, but it was legal." (Therefore, I'm righteous.)

"I'm not hurting anyone else." (Therefore, I'm righteous.)

"Everybody does it. It's normal." (Therefore, I'm righteous.)

"If you knew what I knew, you would do what I did." (I'm righteous.)

"People don't understand me." (Others don't see it, but I'm righteous.)

"Sometimes you just have to do what you have to do." (I'm righteous.)

Self-distraction

It's not always wrong to distract ourselves. We can distract ourselves for good reasons, such as when we need to get our mind off of something we are obsessing about. But self-distraction can also be a way of supporting denial if we are trying to steer our attention away from things that hurt our sense of righteousness. If we don't feel good about how we are behaving at work, for instance, self-distraction can help us avoid thinking about it. This sort of self-distraction doesn't help us; it only helps our feeling of righteousness.

Some of the most common means of self-distraction include: drug abuse, alcohol abuse, eating, talking, working, shopping, surfing the Internet, playing computer games, staying busy and watching television. If we don't feel good about how we are living our life, any of those activities can provide a distraction that helps us avoid thinking about how we are actually living. Some of those activities, such as eating, are necessary, and some may be benign; but any of those activities may be used as a distraction. If we are concerned about whether we are using one of our activities, such as watching television, as a self-distracting strategy of denial, we can test ourselves by trying to abstain from it for a period of time. If we find this is harder than it should be, or we are hesitant to even try the test at all, we may be using the activity as a way of trying to distract ourselves from things that would hurt our feeling of personal righteousness.

We can find all sorts of ways to distract ourselves, some of which may even attract the applause of others. Consider the service of a dedicated professional. Although he may be providing a valuable service to others, he may use that service as a way of occupying his thoughts and energy so that he can avoid thinking about his regrets, his failures, or how he treats his family members. Although his dedication may be much appreciated by those he is serving, he may not be serving them as much as he is serving himself.

Selective Insight

In selective insight, we selectively decide how clearly and intelligently we think about an issue. For instance, it is common to hear someone say, "It's amazing how clearly I can see other people's problems and what they need to do, but when it comes to my own problems, I really struggle." We may be capable of great insight, but our insight is selective. We don't apply the same energy and intelligence to some issues as we do to others. We use our insight if we want to understand something (such as other people's problems and what they need to do) and we withhold it when we don't want to understand something (such as the true nature of our own problems, and what we need to do).

Laziness

Laziness supports denial by keeping reality at a distance. It removes us from the world, idles our thoughts, and shrinks our awareness to our immediate surroundings. There are different kinds of laziness. It isn't always about physical laziness. We can be lazy in our thinking, lazy in our efforts to relate to others, and lazy in our efforts to face up to a demanding situation. Procrastination can be a form of laziness.

Withdrawal

We are all familiar with scenes in which someone leaves the room when they don't want to hear something. We may likewise withdraw when we don't want to hear something that may hurt our feeling of righteousness. Such withdrawal can be accomplished in many ways; we don't necessarily need to withdraw physically. We can simply withdraw from conversation or occupy ourselves with a distraction. We can withdraw emotionally or into our own thoughts. We can withdraw into daydreaming. At times, withdrawal can take a lot of physical, mental or emotional energy. But we may still consider it worth the effort if it helps us maintain a sense of righteousness.

Other Strategies of Denial

There are all sorts of other things we can do to support our denial. These include: joking, threatening, judging, boasting, blaming, controlling a conversation, seeing ourselves as a victim, refusing to think about certain things, spending time with people who support our denial and avoiding people who don't. Each of these things can help us to feel more justified by supporting our denial.

Denial is a Choice

Denial, like all strategies of self-justification, is a choice, a choice that can have serious consequences. Denial can prevent us from seeing our problems and dealing with those problems. It can prevent us from talking about things we need to talk about. It can undermine our personal relationships and endanger our job. Parental denial can spoil a child. Denial about a serious medical condition, an addiction, or the need to take safety precautions, can lead to disability or death.

The grace of God invites us to let go of the denial that supports self-justification. With grace, we can feel free to see ourselves as we are, consider how we are actually living, and think about what we want to do in that light. Without grace, we may not feel free to do any of those things. Grace gives us eyes to see and ears to hear.

We may wonder how we can let go of denial if we don't see what we are in denial about. But denial is usually not a black-and-white thing, as though we are in denial or we are not. Even when it seems total, it is often not; there is still a part of us that knows or at least suspects the truth. It may only be an occasional sense of uneasiness, but it is there. We can look at denial on a scale from 1 to 10, in which a 10 is total denial and a 1 is hardly any denial at all. Even if we are in deep denial, it may not actually be a 10. It may only be an 8 or a 9. Grace allows us to consider even the smallest uneasiness.

Rigidity

Our desire to see ourselves as righteous can lead us to believe things about ourselves and others that help us feel righteous. We may, for instance, believe that we are loyal, caring or diligent because such beliefs help us feel righteous. And we may believe that certain other people are hateful or lazy, because those beliefs help us to feel better about ourselves in comparison.

We can also be motivated to hold beliefs about right and wrong that help us feel righteous; beliefs about our personal relationships that help us feel righteous; beliefs about our workplace that help us feel righteous; beliefs about our religion, or our lack of one, that help us feel righteous; beliefs about our politics, our circumstances, and the world, that help us feel righteous; and beliefs about our grievances, prejudices and opinions that help us feel righteous.

As a result, we can so value our beliefs that we can be rigidly inflexible about them. We can have a self-justifying investment in our beliefs that leads us to hold them tightly. We can be quick to dismiss any evidence against our beliefs, avoid talking about our beliefs with people who may disagree with them, and perceive any threat or challenge to our beliefs as cause for alarm.

It isn't wrong to have a commitment to particular beliefs. Consider the importance of the following beliefs:

It is wrong to murder and steal.
It is wrong to enslave human beings.
It is right to be honest and courageous.
It is right to live with personal integrity.

These are all important beliefs. Rigidity, on the other hand, is a strategy of self-justification in which we are committed to certain beliefs because they support our feeling of righteousness. Consider how the following beliefs can protect or promote a feeling of righteousness:

She'll never learn.
He's just using her.
I've worked hard.
I'm too old to change.
He's hard to talk to.
They're lazy.

Now consider this belief: "If I don't do the dishes, nobody will." Possibly, but possibly not. We may have a self-justifying investment in this belief. It may help us feel mature, responsible, diligent, and better than others. We may say that we would love it if other people helped with the dishes, and we may very much believe our words, but if they did help we might not like it. We may comfort ourselves by thinking that their help won't last, and even look for ways to restore the status quo and the validity of our original belief.

Recognizing Rigidity

We can find rigidity in three basic forms. There is *vehement rigidity, withdrawn rigidity,* and *hit-and-run rigidity*:

- In vehement rigidity, we go on the offensive. We adopt an intimidating posture in which we assert a supreme confidence in our beliefs, forbidding challenge. We say in so many words, "No one had better try to mess with my beliefs! Everyone, if they are wise, should fully agree with my beliefs, or at the very least, keep their mouth shut." There can be painful consequences for those who don't respect our beliefs.

- Withdrawn rigidity looks like classic stubbornness. We believe what we want to believe and that's all there is to it. In this sort of rigidity, we have a tendency to keep our beliefs to ourselves. If our beliefs are challenged, we have no interest in considering the arguments. We may only say, "I know what I know. Don't try to change my mind." Or, "That's just how I am. That's just how I think."

- In hit-and-run rigidity, we assert our beliefs, perhaps even forcefully, but then withdraw if they are challenged. We have no interest in discussing our beliefs with people who disagree with them.

We may not think of ourselves as rigid in our beliefs. We may consign such rigidity to people who seem stubborn, stiff-necked or under-educated. But inasmuch as we withdraw, react angrily when our beliefs are challenged, or keep our beliefs to ourselves out of a concern that they may be tested, we can have a rigid, self-justifying investment in our beliefs.

Truth and Rigidity

Rigidity is similar to denial in that we try to have our own version of the truth. But it is also different from denial. Whereas in denial, we avoid the truth; in rigidity, we fasten onto our own "truth." If someone suggests that we are avoiding the truth, we may comfort ourselves with the belief that we are very committed to the truth (the truth as we see it, and want to see it).

No one has a monopoly on the truth, and it is sometimes difficult to know what is true. But we can find it most difficult to see and understand the truth when we are invested in beliefs that help us feel righteous. Grace, as it frees us from self-justification, frees us from a commitment to self-justifying beliefs. The more we choose grace and let go of self-justification, the more we can see reality as it is. Self-justification obscures the truth. Grace offers clarity.

Life can be challenging and we may wrestle with decisions about work, relationships and responsibilities. Self-justification makes this even harder. Because it leads us to be rigid in our beliefs, it can lead us to have a skewed perception of reality based on those beliefs. The more we choose grace, on the other hand, the better we can find our way. Grace helps us to see where we are now, where we are headed, and where we need to go.

Legalism

Most of us are familiar with legalism. It is based on the belief that we are righteous, justified, acceptable, worthy, when we live up to a particular set of rules or standards. It is an attitude of: "I do this, this and this; therefore, I'm righteous. If you don't do those things, then you're not righteous."

Legalism is often associated with people who are perceived as moralistic, outwardly religious, or hypocritically looking down on others for the way they live. We may also think of prohibitions against dancing, drinking, playing cards or reading certain books. But legalism, as a strategy of self-justification, is not limited to the obvious examples. If we see ourselves as righteous because we do certain things and avoid others, we too are being legalistic.

It is important to have moral standards as well as standards of quality workmanship, academic excellence, and so on. But when we think legalistically, we use our standards as a measure of personal righteousness. Jesus provided an example of legalism in his parable of the Pharisee and the Tax collector. The Pharisee apparently saw himself as righteous and believed that God would see him as righteous because of his adherence to some particular standards. We may have different standards, but we can do the same thing. We too may think of ourselves as a good person because we do certain things and don't do others.

Strategic Advantages of Legalism

Legalism can seem to put us in the driver's seat. Even if we are living by standards that were imposed on us by our culture or upbringing, we still choose the standards that we actually own, and the importance we give to each of those standards. We can be particular about some but not others; and give our attention to some on one day and others on another day. On any given day, we can select the standards with which we measure our righteousness. Consider the analogy of a piano recital. Our performance in a piano recital may be measured by a number of standards, but if we only consider a particular set of standards, we may ignore the rest. We might consider the importance of striking all the right keys in the right order, for instance, but ignore the importance of rhythm or tempo. We may play woodenly, but still feel good about our performance because we only gave importance to striking the right keys in the right order. We can do the same with our moral standards. If we assigned importance to all aspects of our behavior, we might never feel righteous. But if we reserve our focus to only certain things, we may, like the Pharisee, feel righteous. We may see ourselves as righteous because:

- We are loyal to our friends (even though we give little thought to the fact that our loyalty requires us to live with dishonesty).

- We give to charity (even though we give little thought to the fact that we play the Judge and participate in cruel gossip with our friends).

- We go to church every Sunday (even though we give little thought to the fact that we hold rigid beliefs about our grievances).

- We have a strong work ethic (even though we give little thought to the fact that we are neglecting our family).

- We treat some people with love (even though we ignore the fact that we treat others with contempt).

Legalism can also seem like an effective strategy of self-justification because we can be capricious about our judgment of how well our standards are met. We can, for instance, make ourselves the judge of when we are behaving well and when we are not; and we can decide when others are behaving well and when they are not. Sometimes we may think of people as having a double standard. But in legalism, we don't merely have a double standard; our standards, the importance we assign to them, and our judgment of how well they are being met, can all be in continual flux. We can be capricious about our standards according to our best advantage in any particular moment.

Legalism seems to make self-justification more achievable. If we think of ourselves as a good person because we do certain things and refrain from others, then we can see what we need to do in order to feel like a good person.

Consequences of Legalism

Legalism emphasizes the letter of the law over the spirit of the law, and in so doing, leads us to endorse a set of rules for the sake of the rules themselves. Legalism can also:

- Encourage us to fasten on to a particular set of standards that we may hesitate to even question. We may turn a blind eye to the possibility of better standards.

- It can lead us to condemn those who don't meet our standards, which can in turn lead us to be cruel. And although we may give ourselves latitude in our judgment of when we are meeting our standards, we may still at times find it hard to see ourselves as meeting those standards, which can lead to self-condemnation.

- It can lead us to live a life of moral rigidity, timidity and worry; depriving us of the fullness of life that we might otherwise enjoy.

- It can lead us to be less honest about our failures and more likely to ignore important standards when they don't serve our self-justification.

Legalism is a Choice

The grace of God leads us to let go of the legalistic thinking that supports self-justification. Legalism can be a seductive and habitual strategy of self-justification, but it is still a choice. When we think in terms of grace, we have no need for self-justification or the legalistic thinking that seems to support it.

Complicity

Although we can always pursue self-justification independently, we can also work together in our efforts to feel righteous. Consider gossip. In gossip, we complicitly join with others to play the Judge, supporting one another's judgment of a third party. It can be satisfying to play the Judge by ourselves, but it can be all the more satisfying when we work together. We can also complicitly support one another's boasting, denial, and rigid beliefs. We can uphold one another's legalism. And we can help protect one another from the opinions of others who see us as less than righteous.

Self-justification is self-focused, but we can help one another in our pursuit of it.

Consider the following example: If Mary feels doubtful about her righteousness, her complicit friend, Susan, may offer assurances that there is no need to be concerned. She may say something like, "I know you're a good person." If Mary is criticized by Allison, who tells her that she acted badly in a particular situation, Susan, as Mary's complicit friend, may defend Mary, saying, "Never mind what Allison said to you. I think you did fine." Susan may also play the Judge on Mary's behalf, trying to discredit Allison's character. Susan might say, "Don't pay attention to anything Allison says. She's awful!" In complicit relationships, we try to support one another's feeling of righteousness.

A complicit friend can support our goals, approve of our values, defend our attitudes when they come under attack, and validate the appropriateness of our emotions. We may do many of these things in a normal friendship, but in complicit friendships, we do so to help one another feel righteous. If Mary feels angry, for instance, her complicit friend, Susan, may tell Mary that she is "perfectly right" to feel angry, helping Mary feel justified in her anger; and in so doing, helping Mary feel righteous.

We may so value complicity as a strategy of self-justification that we see it as a requirement of friendship. We don't think of people as friends unless they help us feel like a good person; and we see ourselves as being a friend when we help others feel like a good person. We may have little use for those who are not willing to help us feel righteous. And if someone hurts our feeling of righteousness, we may think of that person as an enemy.

We may similarly experience conversations as "good" when they reinforce our feeling of being a good person, and "bad" when they fail to support that feeling. Complicit conversations can leave us feeling good, while the absence of complicity can leave us feeling bored or irritated. We may not think in these terms. We may be unaware of why we experience some conversations as good and others as bad. We may have never given a thought to the concepts of complicity and self-justification. But we can be attracted to people who oblige us with complicity and have little use for those who don't.

Although complicity can provide a sense of closeness, it is not a healthy basis for a friendship. The closeness is dependent upon the strength of the complicity and there may be little or no sense of connection aside from the complicity. Such friendships are similar to the friendships of drug abusers: They feel a sense of camaraderie with one another as they work together to facilitate and justify one another's drug use; but if they lose their usefulness to one another, they may have no more use for one another. Complicit friendships can be the same. If the complicity is lost or abandoned, so may be the friendship. This is not to say that complicity is fragile. We may highly value our complicit friendships and go to great lengths to nurture and preserve them.

We can find complicity among whole groups of people. Like complicit friendships, complicit group members support one another's boasting, judging, denial, rigidity and legalism. They help one another feel righteous, and reassure one another of their righteousness when it is called into question by the words or actions of people outside the group. Complicit groups typically adopt an us-against-them posture in which their complicity separates them from others. They stand together and reassure one another of their superiority to other groups, saying in so many words: "We're the best, the smartest, the strongest, the most stylish (and therefore, the most righteous)."

Complicit groups, like complicit friendships, are not healthy. Group loyalty is often understood as a willingness to cooperate with the (complicit) rules of the group, and group acceptance can be conditional upon that (complicit) cooperation. Those who don't cooperate "don't fit in" and can become targets of persecution and rejection. If we belong to such a group, we can feel pressured in large and small ways to compromise our personal integrity and "play the game."

Inasmuch as complicity is a factor in a group, the viability of that group can depend on that complicity. If the members of such a group work together in consideration of one another's self-justification, there can be harmony and productivity in the group; but if they don't, or worse, they pursue their own self-justification at one another's expense, there can be discord and low productivity. Wherever there are groups, complicity can be present in the groups, and to the extent that it is, the viability of a group can depend on that complicity.

Complicity is a common feature of dysfunctional families. Such families can seem stable when their members support one another's efforts of self-justification; but that apparent stability can disappear when they fail to play by the family's complicit rules. A family can be tightly bonded by a complicity that is valued by each of its members, but at any time those same members may see it as being to their own individual advantage to pursue their self-justification at one another's expense.

If we belong to such a family, we may have some pretty mixed thoughts and feelings about it. On the one hand, we can have an investment in the complicity of our family and a bias in favor of seeing our family and its individual members as good people. If one of our family members is in prison, for instance, we are motivated to believe he was wrongly accused. And if we have a child who was involved in a fight at school, we try not to see her as being at fault. On the other hand, our family complicity is likely only one of our many strategies of self-justification. If we choose, we can abandon it in favor of other strategies and then look at our family very differently. Rather than having a bias in favor of our family and wanting the best for our family members, we take joy in their misfortunes and resent their successes.

Members of dysfunctional families typically play it both ways. They go back and forth from moment to moment between family loyalty and disloyalty, depending upon their current strategy of self-justification. At times, they see their family as the very best of families, but at other times hold it in contempt. Self-justification, not love, is the ruling principle in such a family.

Although complicity can seem like an effective strategy of self-justification, it has some big downsides. It not only fosters unhealthy relationships and pressures us to sacrifice our integrity, it takes away much of our freedom. We can feel tightly bound to our complicit partners, and pressured to walk and talk and even think as they do. If we want to stop gossiping, for instance, we may not feel free to do so as long as our complicit partners want to continue. We can free ourselves by abandoning the complicity, but that may be the last thing we want to do. We not only risk persecution and rejection, we lose one of our strategies of self-justification.

Complicity can sometimes provide a feeling of community and acceptance from others, but it doesn't provide actual community. We are only accepted as an actor on a stage; we are allowed to play a part, and more often than we may want to admit, that is all.

Overbearing

In complicity, we work together to help one another feel justified. In overbearing, we try to *make* people help us feel justified. Although there can be consequences for refusing or breaking complicity, it is still for the most part our choice. We choose to enter into complicity. Overbearing is a strategy of self-justification in which we try to impose complicity. We bear down on those around us to act and even think in ways that support our boasting, legalism, judging, denial and rigidity.

Overbearing can be utilized by fathers, mothers, siblings, bureaucrats, pastors, elders, managers, doctors, or anyone who has some kind of power. We can find it in a family, a church, a workplace, or a party. It may be imposed through anger, a threat of rejection, or even violence. But it isn't necessarily limited to the apparently powerful and it isn't always easy to see how it is happening. Our overbearing can be "nice," while we quietly find ways to punish those who don't cooperate. And instead of using obvious force, we may give people the silent treatment, emotionally withdraw, withhold forgiveness, or withhold respect. We may also find ways to exploit weaknesses, make people feel guilty, or manipulate events from behind the scenes. We may be so clever that people have no idea that they have been coerced.

Overbearing can seem like an effective strategy of self-justification. It may not only help us feel justified, it can help us feel superior to others. And if we live according to the fallacy of 'might makes right' that feeling of superiority helps us feel more righteous than others. As long as we are invested in self-justification, we can be invested in overbearing.

Consequences of overbearing

Overbearing hurts those who practice it, and the people it is practiced upon. But there is one group of people who can be particularly hurt by overbearing, the children of a home in which it is practiced. Consider the following:

- Overbearing can create a fearful environment that punishes personal initiative and discourages people from thinking or speaking for themselves. Children raised in such a home are raised to be submissive to an overbearing authority figure, and as a part of that submission, raised to doubt their own thoughts and feelings in favor of those of an authority figure. Even after growing up and leaving their original family, they may doubt their own perceptions and look for an authority figure to tell them what to think and how they should conduct their lives.

- Overbearing teaches children an unhealthy, one sided way of relating to people in general. Children raised in overbearing families are taught through experience that there are only two ways to be in a relationship: big (fostering dependence in others) or little (being dependent on others). There may be times in any relationship when we need to be the strong one, and there may be times when we find ourselves in need of the strength of others; but if we feel that we must always be in one role or the other, our relationships suffer. Our relationships are healthiest when we normally relate to one another as neither big nor little.

Our Choice

We may feel particularly bad if we see that we have been overbearing, so much so that we feel undeserving of grace. But grace is not something we must deserve. It is a gift that is not dependent on how we have lived or even on how we feel about how we have lived. There is nothing we can do to earn God's grace. It is a gift, a pure gift that has nothing to do with what we deserve.

Abdication

When we first hear the word *abdication* we may think of a king or queen abdicating a thrown. But abdication, as a strategy of self-justification, is something we can all do. In abdication, we abdicate our responsibility for how we are conducting our lives. We abdicate our choice of what we believe, what we value, what we do for work, and how we spend our time. We look for people to speak for us, think for us, and tell us what to do. We can even become a sort of accessory to other people's lives, not living our own life but living as an extension of other people's lives. We become a follower, a member of the "herd" living a life that is far short of the one we might otherwise live.

Abdication keeps us from "showing up." It keeps us from speaking up when we need to speak up, and standing up for what matters when we need to stand up. It keeps us from being the friend that we could be, being the husband or wife that we could be, and being the kind of parent that we could be. It keeps us from being the professional that we could be, and the person we could be. It keeps us from showing up for the life that we could be living.

In the early versions of *A Psychology of Grace*, abdication wasn't referred to by the name 'abdication.' It was only mentioned as "the willing submission to overbearing." Abdication is commonly found in the company of overbearing, and tends to invite overbearing if it is not already present, but it is not dependent on the presence of overbearing. Abdication is a choice, a strategy of self-justification we may use at any time in our pursuit of self-justification.

At first glance, we may wonder why anyone would want to use this strategy of self-justification. But it is actually very popular. If we see someone as an authority, we may also see them as having the authority to decide who is a good person and who is not. Inasmuch as that authority regards us as a person of worth, we can value that regard. Even if it is sparse, capricious or consisting only of tolerance we may find security in it. And if we grew up in a family in which overbearing was a significant part of that home, we may have been raised to only think of ourselves as a person of worth when we felt the approval of an authority figure.

Abdication can also provide an illusion of taking us off the hook. If we allow somebody else to make our decisions for us, we can feel less accountable if something goes wrong. And if we let someone else tell us what we should do, we can feel less responsible if things turn out badly. We may be more than happy to just sort of stand back and let other people take the risks.

And then there is the ease of abdication. Abdication can save us a lot of work. It can be hard to think. It can be hard to make decisions, figure things out, decide what is wise, do the research we need to do, organize our thoughts, talk to certain people, and make the commitments we need to make. It can be hard, even very hard, to find our way in life. Abdication seems to relieve us of a lot of trouble. And if there is an overbearing person trying to control us, giving in can seem like the easy thing to do.

Our Choice

Grace is a choice even in the midst of a lifetime of abdication. There is never a reason we can't choose grace, and there is no one and nothing that can stop us from choosing grace. We can always choose grace, no matter how we feel, no matter how we were raised, and no matter what anyone else thinks.

We don't need to abdicate. We don't need any human authority to tell us that we are a good person. We don't need to evade responsibility, and we don't need to take the road that looks easiest. We can always choose grace. We can choose grace over abdication and every other strategy of self-justification.

Letting go of Self-Justification

Humility is a word that has come into disfavor; once considered a virtue, it is now often associated with weakness, defeat and low self-esteem. But humility is none of those things. It is the willingness to honestly see ourselves as we are, warts and all. It is the choice to live without, or let go of, self-justification.

We don't need to be humbled or humiliated in order to acquire humility. Humility is a choice, the choice to let go of self-justification. Any number of things may prompt us to consider that choice, but it is always and only a choice. We may experience a personal defeat that leaves us feeling "humbled" or we may feel so embarrassed that we are "humiliated," but we may still not choose humility; we may only redouble our efforts of self-justification. We must choose humility, and we do that by choosing to let go of our strategies of self-justification. In the parable of the Tax Collector and the Pharisee, the tax collector chose humility while the Pharisee chose self-justification. It didn't have to be that way. They each could have chosen differently.

The grace of God invites humility. It invites us to let go of self-justification. There many reasons, however, that we may still cling to self-justification. Here are seven of the most common:

1. We don't really understand the grace of God. We see grace only in terms of forgiveness, or in an even more limited sense, forgiveness of particular sins. We liken God to a judge in a court of law; a judge who may grant us leniency for particular sins, but to whom we must still prove ourselves to be a generally good person. We think of ourselves as accountable to this judge, and we believe that he will graciously forgive us for our sins if we sincerely ask. But aside from such humbling occasions, we don't give much thought to grace. We live as we always have, trying to see ourselves as righteous, and trying to prove it. Although we may appeal to the grace of God for particular sins, our lives are still characterized by trying to prove our righteousness. Like the Pharisee who compared himself with the tax collector, we relate to God as a judge, and we want God to see us as righteous.

In a variation of the above, we don't see ourselves as only having to go before God for particular sins; we see ourselves as a sinner. We see sin as a deeply ingrained habit of our lives, entrenched in our attitudes, dispositions and private thoughts. We see God as the gracious Judge who will forgive us for our sinfulness, but aside from this, we don't give much thought to grace. We believe in a God of grace, and believe God will forgive us for our sinfulness, but we still relate to God as a Judge; we want God to see us as righteous and we try to see ourselves as righteous.

It is true that God is our Judge, but it is all the more true that God is our heavenly Father. The grace of God is not merely about the graciousness of our heavenly Judge. It is also about the love of our heavenly Father. Imagine the perfect father. He is not a mere judge of his children. Nor do his children relate to him as a judge, hoping he will see them as righteous and trying to prove their righteousness. He loves his children and they know he loves them. They try to please him but they don't try to make a case for their righteousness. They don't think of him as a judge in a court of law. They think of him as their father.

2. We have a misunderstanding about the nature of grace itself. We think of grace as something that we must earn or deserve. We believe that some people are more worthy of grace than others. But grace is neither earned nor deserved. It is a gift, a true gift. Grace is love as a gift, love as Jesus defined it, in which we love even our enemies. There is no such thing as being found worthy or unworthy of grace. In grace, we are loved and accepted just as we are.

Even if we think of God as our heavenly Father, we may think of a father's love as something we must earn. Our experience with human beings in general may also suggest that love must be earned. We believe we must prove ourselves worthy of good things. But grace is love as a gift, a love that is not and cannot be earned. We don't need to prove ourselves worthy of grace.

3. We understand that grace is a gift that cannot be earned. But we also believe, at least in practice, that God's grace is insufficient; it only takes us so far. We believe that God has come incredibly far to reach us but we must still somehow make up the remaining distance. Although we profess a faith in the grace of God, we don't really believe in it, and we continue to live a life of self-justification.

4. We don't want to be dependent upon God's grace. We want to stand on our own, on our own merit, without any "crutches." We may avail ourselves of God's grace when we feel like we don't have any other choice, but that may be the last thing we want to do. We don't like the feeling of having to humble ourselves. We want to be self-sufficient, independent, and righteous in our own right. We like to think of ourselves as better than others, more righteous than others, and sometimes, even more righteous than God. We don't want to humble ourselves before God or anyone else. Nor do we want to owe God, or anyone, anything.

Though we may not admit it, we want to be great, and we want to prove ourselves worthy of honor. We want glory, praise, fame, credit, applause. We don't want grace. We want to keep score, and we want to win. So although we may avail ourselves of the grace of God if we must, we want to avoid such occasions if we can. And if we can't, we very much want to forget about them afterwards and regain our sense of prideful self-sufficiency.

5. We continue to employ strategies of self-justification out of inertia. Long-standing habits of self-justification can characterize our lives. Just as we may drive our car without giving much thought to what we are doing, we can practice strategies of self-justification without giving much thought to what we are doing. Although we may profess a belief in the grace of God, we think as we have always thought, behave as we have always behaved, and relate to others as we have always related to them. We live with inertia and continue to employ our habitual strategies of self-justification. We may

adopt some new beliefs and change some of our habits, but we mostly live as we have always lived without giving it much thought.

At first glance, inertia may appear to be a failure to live purposely. It is as though we are just sort of living on automatic, going through each day without really thinking about what we are doing. But inertia itself is a choice, a choice to live thoughtlessly. We choose to refrain from giving much thought to what we are doing or how we are really living. We choose safe activities that distract us from things we don't want to think about. We choose idle chatter rather than serious conversation. And we make those choices because they help protect our feeling of being a good person. If we did not feel righteous, we would not feel so comfortable; we would feel restless, irritated. We would move out of our inertia. We would do something different. But for the time being, we feel justified, and that's how we like it, so we stay where we are. When we live with inertia, we are not failing to live purposely; we actually do have a purpose. Our purpose is self-justification, and our inertia supports that purpose.

6. We have a good understanding of self-justification, but we are only looking at how other people are doing it. We may see self-justification everywhere we look and be disgusted by it and distraught about it, but then only use this awareness to play the Judge. We judge others for their self-justification but look away from our own.

7. We have a good understanding of self-justification and of why we need to let go of it, but we still find ourselves drawn to it because it seems so rewarding. Self-justification

can help us feel better about ourselves, and at times persuade others to think more highly of us too. It can help us feel more righteous than others, and protect us from things that might hurt our feeling of righteousness. It can provide a powerful illusion of connection and community, and deliver us from any feeling of responsibility for how we are living our life.

Self-justification can also provide a sense of meaning and purpose. It may be one of the things we live for: the hope of somehow proving ourselves a person worthy of love and respect. That hope can guide our personal values, direct our thoughts, determine how we relate to others, and influence our long-term goals. Self-justification can play a large part in our lives; it is not enough to simply remove it. We must replace it with a new way of living.

2

Living with Grace

A lawyer stood up to put [Jesus] to the test, saying, "Teacher, what shall I do to inherit eternal life?" He said to him, "What is written in the Law? How do you read it?" And he answered, "You shall love the Lord your God with all your heart and with all your soul and with all your strength and with all your mind, and your neighbor as yourself." And he said to him, "You have answered correctly; do this, and you will live." But he, desiring to justify himself, said to Jesus, "And who is my neighbor?" Jesus replied, "A man was going down from Jerusalem to Jericho, and he fell among robbers, who stripped him and beat him and departed, leaving him half dead. Now by chance a priest was going down that road, and when he saw him he passed by on the other side. So likewise a Levite, when he came to the place and saw him, passed by on the other side. But a Samaritan, as he journeyed, came to where he was, and when he saw him, he had compassion. He went to him and bound up his wounds, pouring on oil and wine. Then he set him on his own animal and brought him to an inn and took care of him. And the next day he took out two denarii and gave them to the innkeeper, saying, 'Take care of him, and whatever more you spend, I will repay you when I come back.' Which of these three, do you think, proved to be a neighbor to the man who fell among the robbers?" He said, "The one who showed him mercy." And Jesus said to him, "You go, and do likewise." (The Gospel of Luke, chapter 10, verses 25-37)

Jesus told this parable, not as an example of God's grace, but as an example of human grace. Just as God has demonstrated grace toward us, we can live with grace toward one another. And not only is this something we can do, it is something that we are directed to do. Jesus made this point in another parable about a man who was forgiven a large debt by his king but then failed to forgive the much smaller debt that another man owed to him (Matthew 18:23-35). The parable concludes with the king asking the first debtor, *Should not you have had mercy on your fellow servant, as I had mercy on you?* Just as God is merciful to us, we can be merciful to one another. Jesus made this plain when he said, *Be merciful, even as your [heavenly] Father is merciful* (Luke 6:36).

The apostle Paul likewise wrote:

- *Be kind to one another, tenderhearted, forgiving one another, as God in Christ forgave you.* (Ephesians 4:32)
- *Put on then, as God's chosen ones, holy and beloved, compassionate hearts, kindness, humility, meekness, and patience, bearing with one another and, if one has a complaint against another, forgiving each other; as the Lord has forgiven you, so you also must forgive. And above all these put on love, which binds everything together in perfect harmony.* (Colossians 3:12-14)
- *Let your speech always be gracious, seasoned with salt.* (Colossians 4:6)

And the apostle John wrote:

- *Whoever says he abides in him ought to walk in the same way in which he walked.* (1 John 2:6)
- *Beloved, if God so loved us, we also ought to love one another.* (1 John 4:11)

Grace is sometimes understood as love flowing downward, the love of the greater for the lesser, such as God's love toward us or the love of the father toward his wayward son in the parable of the Prodigal Son. But there is no reason to think of grace as flowing downward alone. We can also understand grace as the love we extend to one another without any consideration of who is above whom, who is greater than whom, who is more righteous than whom, or who owes whom.

Grace may also be seen as an exceptional thing. We may only associate it with the lives of saints or with God alone. But we can all live with grace; we can all choose to think and act with grace. Each of us may be able to remember times when, even though we were as mad as a hornet, we knew that we could act with grace if we chose. Maybe we did and maybe we didn't, but we knew, or at least knew later, that the choice was ours.

Just as Jesus painted a picture of God's grace in his parable of the Prodigal Son, he painted a picture of the grace we can extend to one another in his parable of the Good Samaritan. Grace is not merely an act of God. We can all think and speak and act with grace.

We can therefore choose grace in two basic ways: as we saw in the last chapter, we can choose God's grace over self-justification; and as we will now consider in this chapter, we can choose to regard one another with grace.

We have already looked at some of the reasons for choosing God's grace over self-justification: we can see our life more clearly; we can find a greater freedom to let go of judging and the competition over who is more righteous than whom; we can find a greater freedom to let go of complicit and overbearing relationships... There is much good that can come from simply letting go of self-justification. But the grace of God leads us to do more than let go of self-justification. It also leads us to live with grace ourselves, extending God's grace to one another. As we do, we find more reasons to choose grace, reasons that can bring new meaning to our lives and strengthen our choice to let go of self-justification. In this and the following chapter, we will look at what it means to live with grace, how we can choose to live with grace, and some of the many reasons to live with grace. Consider some of the most basic reasons:

- We can find our compass in life, along with a stronger sense of who we are as a person.

- We can learn what it means to be a real person and how we can become more of a real person, *real* in the sense of not pretending, not playing games, not playing a role.

- We can learn what it means to have healthy relationships, and how we can have healthier relationships than we do now.

Our grace can take many forms. The following pages look at *generosity, compassion, forgiveness, respect* and *love* as expressions of grace; and how *gumption* and *spirituality* can characterize a life of grace.

Generosity

There are all sorts of gifts. There are Christmas gifts, birthday gifts, wedding gifts, graduation gifts, and gifts for no particular occasion. There are gifts of time, gifts of personal attention, and gifts of service. Affection, kind words, and complements can be gifts. A gift has two qualities: it is good and it is free. There is no expectation of return, leverage or advantage for the giver. A gift, as an expression of grace, is a celebration of life, love, and our relationships with one another; it adds to the joy and fullness of life.

When we don't think in terms of grace, we don't think of gifts as truly gifts. We believe that all things must be earned or deserved, including gifts. We also believe that gifts create an obligation in the recipient; and we give our gifts with an expectation of some kind of return. We have a tendency to "keep score" and if we are given a gift we can be uncomfortable until "we are even." If someone gives us a gift and we resist it because we don't think we deserve it, we are not thinking in terms of grace.

Consider the following example: A man gives flowers to his wife, saying that he loves her and just wants to give her flowers. In other words, they are simply a gift. She is suspicious. It's not her birthday or Valentine's Day or their anniversary. She wonders what he is trying to achieve. Is he looking for a special favor? Is he feeling guilty about something? Does he want something? Time goes by and she never discovers the reason for the flowers. She begins to think that maybe they were just a gift. Then she starts to feel like she owes him something in return. She also likes to think of herself as more righteous than her husband, and his gift of flowers seems to elevate his righteousness above hers. This makes her uncomfortable, and she wants to do something to even the score, or even better, help her feel like she is once again the better person.

When we don't think in terms of grace, we fail to receive a gift as a gift, and our own gifts are not truly gifts. If we are in a competition over who is more righteous than whom, for instance, we may only give a gift with the goal of winning the upper hand in the competition. And if we think we are losing the competition, we may only give a gift with the goal of evening the score. We may also avoid any thought of giving a gift because, in a competition over who is more righteous than whom, the giving of a gift can feel like giving points to the competition. We may likewise compare the value of our gifts with the value of other people's gifts, and then look down on them if we think of our gifts as more valuable than theirs.

When we think in terms of grace, on the other hand, we accept a gift as a gift, and our own gifts are truly gifts. Some may say that there is no such thing as a pure and simple gift, not in human relationships anyway; but the more we think in terms of grace, the more our gifts are truly gifts.

There is a common misunderstanding about generosity: the belief that, since it is an act of grace, we should not consider how our gift may be used; our gift should come with no questions asked. When we think in terms of grace, however, we don't lay all judgments aside. We don't play the Judge, but we still make judgments about trust, morality, ability and quality. Neglecting such judgments can lead to trouble. A gift is meant to enhance life; it is meant to save, maintain, build, strengthen and celebrate life. If we don't consider how our gifts may be used we can do more harm than good. Even with careful thought, our gifts may still at times do harm; but if we give gifts carelessly, we are not being generous, we are being inconsiderate. Real gifts require adequate thought.

Enabling

Inconsiderate gift giving can lead to enabling. Although we may usually associate the word *enabling* with the idea of enabling alcoholics to continue drinking, we can enable many unhealthy things. In addition to enabling an addiction, we can enable dependency, irresponsibility, immaturity, and bad behavior in general. Examples of enabling include:

- Doing for others what they need to be doing for themselves, such as picking up a child's toys when he is old enough to do it himself, or trying to find a job for a grown child who is doing little or nothing to find one for herself.

- Providing the means to continue unhealthy behavior, such as giving an addict money that he will likely use to buy drugs or alcohol.

- Rescuing others from the consequences of their actions, such as bailing someone out of jail for the fourth time.

If we give a gift without really considering how it may be used, and it is then used wrongly, we may console ourselves by thinking that our intentions were good. We may justify ourselves by saying, "I know I should have given it more thought, but my heart was in the right place." But it may also be true that our heart was actually in the wrong place. Strategies of self-justification such as denial and rigidity can keep us from really thinking about the possible impact of our gift. And a desire to boast, even if only to ourselves, can lead us astray as well. The more we let go of self-justification and think in terms of grace, the more our gifts are truly gifts.

Generosity as a Choice

We can choose to think of our gifts as simply gifts. We can choose to give gifts without consideration of whether they are earned or deserved. We can choose to give gifts without looking for some kind of return or advantage. And we can choose to refrain from "keeping score" or otherwise thinking of gifts as game pieces in a competition over who is more righteous than whom. These are all choices. We can likewise choose to be thoughtful about our gifts: thoughtful about our motivations and thoughtful about the appropriateness of our gifts. We can choose to think and act with grace.

Compassion

Compassion is a gift of mercy, acceptance, encouragement and help; it offers hope, warmth, strength and healing to those in pain. When we think in terms of grace, we don't think of compassion as something that must be deserved. Nor do we think of ourselves as better than those who are suffering. Our thoughts, words and actions are characterized by grace. We don't expect a return, and we don't play the Judge. When the Good Samaritan saw the injured man in the road, "he had compassion."

Jesus didn't say anything about the identity of that man who had fallen among robbers. He didn't say anything about his race, social rank or office. He didn't say anything about his righteousness or unrighteousness, or about what he may or may not have deserved. He was just a person who had fallen among robbers. The priest and Levite evidently regarded him as unworthy of their compassion. The Samaritan responded differently.

When we don't think in terms of grace, we may simply be annoyed by the suffering of others or dismiss their suffering as deserved. But inasmuch as we are also invested in self-justification, we may take advantage of their suffering to enhance our feeling of righteousness. Consider the following:

- We can use other people's suffering as an opportunity to play the Judge, to imagine and gossip about what someone must have done to deserve such suffering. Even if we don't see any reason for someone's suffering, we may find satisfaction in thinking that they must have done something to deserve it. We may even like to think that if they had lived righteously, like ourselves, they would not have been afflicted with such suffering.

- We can use other people's suffering as an opportunity to play the Servant, which can help us feel righteous. If we do a good job, we may also be viewed as a "savior" or an "angel" by those we serve.

- We can use other people's suffering as an opportunity for our pity, which can help us feel superior to others and therefore more righteous than others. Our pity can also masquerade as compassion, which can make us seem all the more righteous.

- We can use other people's suffering as a distraction from things we don't want to think about, things that might hurt our feeling of righteousness.

True compassion, on the other hand, does not dismiss those in need as deserving their suffering. Nor does it look for a self-justifying pay-off. It is a gift of grace.

There may be times when people apparently do deserve their suffering, such as a drunk driver who hurts himself while also hurting others, or a child who fails a test at school because she didn't study. But when we think in terms of grace, we don't play the Judge; our compassion is not contingent upon anyone's behavior. It can take different forms depending on our judgment of how we should appropriately respond, but our compassion is unconditional.

When we find it hard to be compassionate because people seem to deserve their suffering, we may find the reason in where we are looking. Consider the following example: A man weighing close to 400 pounds is having trouble getting around his home and even meeting his basic needs. We know that the man has contributed to his weight gain in many ways and is still doing so. Knowing this, we can find it hard to be compassionate, but we can find our way clear when we reconsider our focus. Instead of focusing on his behavior, we can focus on his soul; the soul of a man who may be lost and in pain in more ways than he or anyone else knows.

Compassion, like generosity, requires thought. Just as inconsiderate gifts can create problems, so can inconsiderate attempts to help people in pain. There may be times, for instance, when we are too quick to alleviate pain, robbing people of an opportunity to learn from the consequences of their actions. And if we make a practice of this, we may give people the impression that they don't need to be careful about what they do because someone will likely rescue them if they get into trouble. Compassion, like generosity, must be thoughtful.

Even when we think in terms of grace, it can be hard to know how to offer compassion. Consider the example of offering a listening ear: There may be times when it is helpful to offer a listening ear. Someone may need to work something out, simply feel heard, or find comfort in realizing that he or she is not alone. At other times, however, offering a listening ear can be unhelpful. It may only provide an apparently sympathetic ear for rationalization, gossip, or some other form of self-justification. It can be hard to know whether we should offer a listening ear or not. Our own self-justification, however, can make this challenge even harder. Self-justification distorts our priorities, leading us to be more focused on our own needs rather than the needs of others. Returning to the example of the listening ear, self-justification can lead us to offer that ear even though it would not be good. We may, for instance, offer a listening ear because we fear that if we don't, we could lose the approval of the person who wants that ear. We may also offer a listening ear because doing so helps us to think of ourselves as compassionate, and therefore righteous. On the other side of the coin, self-justification may lead us to not want to listen even though it would be helpful. We may not want to listen because we don't want to be bothered, or we may be afraid of hearing something that would hurt our feeling of righteousness.

Compassion as a Choice

Grace is a choice, a choice we can make at any time. And compassion, as an expression of grace, is a choice we can make at any time as well. When we think in terms of grace, we don't think of compassion as something that needs to be earned or deserved. We think of it as an unconditional gift, a gift we can even extend to those who lie to us, those who hate us, and those who hurt us. We can always, in any moment, think about those who are suffering with compassion; and we can always, in any moment, speak and act with compassion.

Everyday Compassion

Compassion is often only thought of as an occasional response to sickness, weakness or some kind of emotional pain. But compassion is most frequently needed, even to the extent that it is needed daily, as a response to other people's efforts of self-justification. Self-justification can be understood as an expression of pain, spiritual pain. It is painful to feel less than righteous, especially so if there is no hope of grace. We may therefore liken self-justification to the restless thrashing about of a suffering person on a sickbed. Picture it. Picture someone moving around restlessly on a sickbed, sometimes even violently, trying to find relief from pain. If "thrashing" doesn't seem to capture how someone is acting, we may think of someone curled up in a ball, face tight and fists clenched. Just as we can respond with compassion when we see people trying to find relief from physical or emotional pain, we can respond with compassion when we see people trying to find relief from their spiritual pain.

Consider the boasting of others, which we may find annoying and even exasperating. We may also be tempted to play the Judge or see ourselves as better than the person who is boasting. But a boastful person can be likened to someone who is suffering from physical pain and trying to feel better. The suffering in this case is not physical, it is spiritual, but the pain is just as real. Boasting can be seen as an attempt to ameliorate the spiritual pain that comes with a feeling of unrighteousness. We may respond with self-justified annoyance when we are confronted with boasting, or we can respond with compassion.

We can likewise respond with compassion when someone is trying to take refuge in rationalization or self-distraction. We can respond with compassion when we see someone is in denial. We can respond with compassion when we see people abdicating or sacrificing their integrity. And we can even respond with compassion when people are judging us, gossiping about us, putting us down, or otherwise trying to see themselves as above us or better than us. In each case, we can picture someone suffering and trying to find relief for their spiritual pain. Jesus told his disciples to love their enemies. This perspective sheds light on how we can actually do that.

It hurts to be judged, misunderstood and unfairly criticized. It's hard to be around people who are legalistic or rigid in their thinking. It's hard to be around people who are angry and overbearing, but an understanding of self-justification can show us a bigger picture. The world is full of people who are hurting, not just with physical or emotional pain, but with spiritual pain. Their strategies of self-justification can be understood as attempts to find relief from that pain. We may not feel like responding with compassion, but when we choose to think in terms of grace, we always can.

This is true even in how we regard ourselves. It can be tempting to condemn ourselves when we see our own self-justification. But just as it is wrong to sit in judgment of others, and whether they deserve compassion, it is also wrong to sit in judgment of ourselves, and whether we deserve compassion. Just as we can extend grace to others, God regards us with grace.

Forgiveness

Then Peter came up and said to him, "Lord, how often will my brother sin against me, and I forgive him? As many as seven times?" Jesus said to him, "I do not say to you seven times, but seventy times seven." (Matthew 18:21-22)

It's natural to feel angry when we have been hurt by someone. It's natural to have our emotions stirred deeply and painfully when we see or experience injustice. When we think in terms of grace, we can forgive those responsible and release those feelings; when we are invested in self-justification, on the other hand, we can find it hard or seemingly impossible to do either.

There is a lot of confusion about forgiveness. We each seem to have an intuitive sense of what it is, and of how important it is, but it is a hard word to define. We may best begin to understand forgiveness by looking at how self-justification leads us to hold on to our grievances:

- We can feel judged when we are treated badly. We can feel as though we were found unworthy of respect and treated accordingly. We may then respond by attempting to discredit the person who treated us badly, trying to paint that person as a bad person, a person whose judgment doesn't count. This can lead us to hold onto our grievances as evidence against that person's character.

- If we are invested in a competition over who is more righteous than whom, we are motivated to keep a tally of the bad things our opponent has done; we want to hold on to the grievances that testify against our opponent's righteousness; and we want to hold on to all that seems to support those grievances such as our anger, our judgments, our perceptions, and self-pity. As long as we can keep our opponent "in the doghouse" we can feel as though we are winning the competition over who is more righteous than whom.

- If someone has acted badly and made themselves a target for our judgment, we can feel as though we have the right to play the Judge. And inasmuch as we enjoy that role, we can be invested in holding on to the grievances that seem to give us that right.

Grievances can also seem to support self-justification in other ways. They can help offset a sense of personal guilt. They can provide a distraction from things we don't want to deal with. They can seem to justify our sloth or rigidity. They can seem to validate our legalism. Sharing our grievances with a third party can help us create or strengthen a sense of complicity.

A Definition of Forgiveness

In light of the ways in which self-justification can motivate us to hold onto and even nurture our grievances, we can understand forgiveness as involving the choice to let go of, or refrain from, making use of the self-justifying opportunities that present themselves when we experience a grievance. If we have been playing the Judge, forgiveness is the decision to stop. If we have been playing the game of who is more righteous than whom, it is the decision to stop playing that game. If we are holding on to our grievances because they seem to justify our denial or rigidity, it is the decision to let go.

In forgiveness, we let go of self-justification; we are no longer invested in grievances and we can let them go. Our feelings may still take time to subside, and we may need time to work through our thoughts about a grievance, but we no longer have the same investment in it. We can let our emotional pain go as it is ready to go. We may be out-raged or furious, but we have no self-justifying investment in those feelings. No matter how badly we have been hurt, our choice to let go of self-justification allows us to let go of our pain.

Forgiveness, however, is not simply a matter of letting go of grievances. It also involves a change in our attitude toward those who have hurt us; the kind of change we make when we replace resentment with grace. Forgiveness leads us to think about those who have hurt us with grace, speak to them with grace, and speak of them with grace.

We can therefore think of forgiveness as having two components: the choice to refrain from using grievances in support of self-justification, and the choice to regard offend-ers with grace. In short, *forgiveness* may best be defined as the choice of grace over self-justification when confronted with a grievance.

Without grace, we may not even consider forgiveness. We may still consider it as a means of reconciling our estranged relationships or improving our mental health, but we may also be so invested in our grievances that we don't want to forgive no matter how much pain it brings into our lives. We may not forgive even little things until we choose grace.

Misunderstandings about Forgiveness

Like other expressions of grace, there are some common misunderstandings about forgiveness: *forgetting* is sometimes seen as a necessary part of forgiveness; *apologies* are often seen as a requirement for forgiveness; and forgiveness is often understood as a *process* that takes time rather than a choice we can make at all times.

Forgetting

There is a common belief that forgiveness necessarily includes forgetting, as in the old saying, "forgive and forget." But there is no necessary connection between forgiving and forgetting, and there may be times when it is important that we don't forget. As an analogy, if a child is sprayed by a skunk, she can forgive the skunk, but she has learned an important lesson; one that she shouldn't forget. If she is wise, she will remember the lesson and give skunks more distance in the future. If she forgets, she may get too close again and get sprayed again. The same can apply to a human relationship. If we are hurt by someone, the experience can teach us to be more careful in the future. Perhaps we have been giving that person too much trust. We can always forgive, but there are times when we are unwise to forget.

When Jesus told the parable of the Prodigal Son, he did not include forgetting with forgiveness. The wayward son in the parable was instantly forgiven by his father, with love and celebration; but he had squandered his share of his father's possessions and his father did not forget. At the end of the parable, he reassures his other son, the one who had stayed at home, that his remaining possessions would go to him. They were not to be divided again. He told him, "All that is mine is yours." He forgave his wayward son, but he did not forget what he had done. If he had included forgetting with forgiving and divided his possessions between his sons again, he would have been unjust.

In forgiveness, we let go of our grievances and regard those who have hurt us with grace. None of that requires us to forget. Like the father of the prodigal son, we can forgive without forgetting and our forgiveness is no less real.

The belief that forgiving must include forgetting can lead us to not even want to consider forgiveness. We may be rightly concerned that if we forget, that could allow us to be hurt again. And we may rightly fear that forgetting bad behavior could encourage that behavior to continue. Such forgetting may not only allow repeated injustice; it can allow continued irresponsibly, laziness, recklessness, and immaturity. At times, it may be safe and even wise to forget, but at other times, we may very much need to remember.

Someone may say, "If you really forgive me, then you should be willing to forget." But forgiveness and forgetting are two different things. People with whom we are complicit may pressure us to forget, and those who are overbearing can insist upon it, but forgiveness does not require us to forget.

Apologies

There is also some confusion about whether forgiveness depends upon repentance or at least an apology. Apologies are helpful. They can help to restore trust in a relationship. But forgiveness, as an act of grace, is not dependent upon what anyone else does. It is not something that must be earned or deserved. It is a gift of grace. If we require an apology before we forgive, then we make our forgiveness conditional.

With grace, forgiveness is not dependent upon an apology. Nor is it dependent upon repentance. Trust suffers without repentance, but we can always forgive. Consider the basic elements of forgiveness: We can choose to refrain from judging, and if we have been judging we can stop. We can choose to refrain from using an offense as grist for the mill of our self-justification in any way. And we can choose to regard those who have offended us with grace. We can do all of those things without first getting an apology.

Practically speaking, making our forgiveness dependent upon an apology can even prevent us from forgiving. Apologies can be hard to come by. When they do come, they can be insincere, and some people may refuse to apologize at all. If we make our forgiveness dependent upon an apology, especially a sincere apology, we not only make our forgiveness conditional, we prevent ourselves from forgiving until our conditions are met. We surrender our ability to forgive to the very people who have caused us pain, people we may now have less reason to trust. Making our forgiveness dependent upon an apology can also prevent us from forgiving people who are not available, such as those who have died.

With grace, we can forgive people even when they are not open to hearing about their offense. And we can forgive them even if they continue to offend us. Our forgiveness is not contingent upon the attitude or behavior of anyone, no matter who they are and no matter how they are treating us. Our forgiveness is a gift of grace.

Process

Some believe that forgiveness is a process, and that it takes time to forgive. It is true that it can take time to work through our thoughts and feelings about an offense, and it can take time for trust to rebuild when it is betrayed. But these things are not to be confused with forgiveness itself. Forgiveness, as an act of grace, is a choice to let go of our investment in grievances and regard those who have hurt us with grace. This is not a process; it is a choice, a choice we can make at any time. Rather than thinking of forgiveness as a process, we can think of it as the choice that allows a process, the process of working through our painful thoughts and feelings.

Without forgiveness, we may have no interest in working through our thoughts and feelings about an offense. We may have no interest in rebuilding trust. We may instead be invested in making a case against the person who has hurt us. Rather than working through our thoughts and emotions, we may be more interested in holding on to our grievances and fanning the flames of our anger. We must first forgive. Then we can work through our pain constructively.

Sometimes forgiveness does seem to be a process in that we may go back and forth between grace and self-justification. At times we are forgiving and at other times unforgiving. Still, forgiveness as an act of grace is a choice, a choice that doesn't require a process. We may need to choose forgiveness again and again, but this is not a process. It is simply a repeated choice we make when we find ourselves falling back into the ways of self-justification.

Forgiveness as a Choice

Unforgiveness can have serious consequences. It can wreak havoc in our relationships; and open a door to disrespect, contempt and cruelty. It can take a toll on our emotional and physical health, and lead us to make some very bad decisions. It can leave us with feelings of fury, sadness, hate, self-pity, anxiety, fatigue, or just a raw ache deep within us. It can nurture all sorts of pain, pain that may seem relentless until we forgive.

We may not feel like forgiving; we may *very* much not feel like forgiving, but the choice is always ours and we can if we choose. Although our anger may be fresh, seething and unabated, we can still forgive. Just as grace is always and in every moment a choice, forgiveness is always and in every moment a choice.

Respect

Jesus showed respect to a Samaritan woman (John 4) in at least three ways that were unusual for the time. First, she was a woman, and women were not considered worthy of respect unless they were associated with men who commanded respect. Secondly, she was a Samaritan, a race that was deemed unworthy of respect. And third, she had had five husbands, and she was not married to the man with whom she was currently living. For any one of these reasons, she would have been considered unworthy of respect. Yet in all that Jesus said, he spoke to her with respect. At other times, he also showed an unusual respect for children, sinners, lepers, the poor, and tax collectors; all people who were not normally regarded with respect.

Respect is a hard word to define. It is not just being courteous, considerate, friendly, fair, nice or deferential. It is something different, something deeper than any of those things; respect touches our soul and acknowledges our true humanity. Some people define *respect* with the Golden Rule: *As you wish that others would do to you, do so to them* (Luke 6:31). That has a lot of truth to it, but it still doesn't really capture the full idea of respect. Examples of disrespect come to mind more easily. We can see disrespect in malicious name calling, sarcasm, yelling, impatience, ignoring, sneering, lying, eye rolling, and in all sorts of abuse. We can even see disrespect in a subtle look, a tone or a gesture.

Most of us seem to have an intuitive idea of respect. Although we may not be able to define it, we know what it is. When we're honest with ourselves, we know when we're treating someone with respect and we know when we're not. It seems that we simply know. Although respect can be hard to define, our basic human awareness of it is strong. When disrespect is allowed in a relationship it is not because it is unrecognized; it is because someone is believed to be deserving of it.

Respect may best be understood as a kind of everyday grace, the common grace we can extend to one another as a general attitude. Grace is sometimes seen as a special gift reserved for special times. But there is no reason to reserve grace for special times. We can adopt a general attitude of grace toward one another at all times. We can think about one another with grace, speak to one another with grace, and relate to one another with grace as a normal practice.

Respect, as a gift of grace, is unconditional. It is not contingent upon anyone's race, sex, age, money, social position, or apparent righteousness. It is not contingent upon how people have behaved or on what they have achieved. Nor is it contingent upon how we expect them to behave. It is not contingent upon anything. It is a gift of grace.

Without grace, personal respect is typically understood as conditional: we believe that people must be found worthy of respect in order to be granted respect. Our respect has conditions. It must be deserved. This is how many of us were taught to understand respect, and we may be used to hearing people say things like:

"I'll treat you with respect when you earn it. Respect is earned."

"I'll treat you with respect when you treat me with respect."

"You don't deserve respect."

That is one way of talking about respect. But we can also make our respect a gift of grace that has nothing to do with what anyone deserves.

Misunderstandings about Respect

There are some common misunderstandings about respect:

1. Respecting a person is sometimes understood as the same as respecting that person's behavior. But these are two different things. We can respect someone as a person without respecting that person's behavior. If people do things we

don't respect it doesn't mean that they are worthy of personal disrespect. Even if people commit terrible crimes and we deplore their behavior, we can still regard them with personal respect; and doing so doesn't mean that we approve of their behavior. With grace, we can regard people with respect regardless of what they have done or how they have lived. We can even regard people with respect when they treat us with disrespect. Our respect for people is not dependent on their behavior. It is a gift of grace.

2. Respect is sometimes confused with trust. But trust and respect are also two different things. Although we can think of personal respect as unconditional, there is no reason to think the same about trust. Trust is based on what we expect someone to do, which can be contingent upon any number of things. Jesus regarded trust as conditional. He didn't extend unconditional trust to others, and he didn't encourage his followers to do so. To the contrary, he told them to beware of certain people, saying for instance, *Watch and beware of the leaven of the Pharisees and Sadducees* (Matthew 16:6; in other words, *Watch and beware of the teaching and social influence of the Pharisees and Sadducees,* the cultural authorities of the day). Although our respect is unconditional, our trust can depend on a number of things.

Trust and respect are often seen as necessarily bound together, as though it is wrong to have one without the other. We may hear someone say, "If you respect me then you should trust me." But trust is its own issue. We can respect people without trusting them. We can respect a child, for instance, without trusting that child to behave. Trust is based upon our expectations of whether someone can be relied upon to act in a certain way. It has little to do with grace. With grace, we can give someone opportunities to earn our trust, but our trust is still conditional upon what we expect that person to do.

Decisions about trust can be one of the most challenging aspects of any relationship. But that has nothing to do with personal respect. We can respect people no matter how much or how little we trust them. Personal respect is an expression of grace that is independent of trust.

3. Respect is sometimes seen as a sign of weakness. Those who are weak are expected to show respect to those who are strong. The powerful, on the other hand, are often not expected to show respect; treating others with disrespect, and getting away with it, is not uncommon among those with power. When we think in terms of grace, however, we don't think of respect as something that must be earned or deserved; we think of it as a gift, a gift of grace that has nothing to do with anyone's power or position.

4. Respect is sometimes understood as being nice or complicit, and that being otherwise is disrespectful. It may even be understood as a willingness to submit to overbearing. We may believe that it is disrespectful "to make waves," and that we should say nothing that might upset someone. But respect doesn't require us to avoid upsetting anyone. We can be respectful while speaking the truth. We can be respectful while having firm boundaries. We can be respectful while taking an unpopular stand. And we can be respectful while saying painful things. It is not disrespectful to have our own ideas, values and opinions. Nor is it disrespectful to express

them. We can be disrespectful in how we express them, but we can also be respectful.

Respect as a Choice

Respect is essential in personal relationships. Disrespect, on the other hand, is one of the quickest and surest ways to hurt or even destroy a relationship. And although we may think of conditional respect as preferable to outright disrespect, it is also toxic to relationships; although it may not end a relationship, it often leads to relationships characterized by manipulation, stress, dependency, stagnation, despair, a feeling of distance, and at times violence.

Grace is a choice, a choice we can make at any time. And respect, as an expression of grace, is a choice we can make at any time as well. When we think in terms of grace, we don't regard one another with respect because we think it is deserved, nor do we regard one another with respect merely because we think we should; we regard one another with respect because we think of personal respect as something that is unconditional.

Self-respect

If it has been our custom to think of respect as conditional, it may seem natural to think of self-respect as conditional. Just as we may regard one another with conditional respect, we may regard ourselves with conditional respect, believing that we do not deserve respect unless we have somehow earned it. But just as we can regard one another with unconditional respect as a choice, we can regard ourselves with unconditional respect as a choice.

When we regard one another with grace, we don't set ourselves up as a Judge of who is worthy of respect and who is not. Our respect is unconditional, and we have no reason to make any exceptions. In this light, our self-respect, like our respect for others, is also unconditional. We don't set ourselves up as a Judge of when we are worthy of respect and when we are not. Our self-respect is not contingent upon our race, sex, age, money, social position or apparent righteousness. Nor is it contingent upon how we have behaved, what we have achieved, or what anyone thinks of us. Even if we see that we have done something wrong, we can admit it and deal with the consequences while at the same time treating ourselves with respect.

Conditional self-respect is commonly known as *self-esteem*. If we judge ourselves worthy of respect, we have high self-esteem. And if we don't judge ourselves worthy of respect, we have low self-esteem. Self-esteem has been emphasized as an essential of mental health. We may think of trying to improve a child's self-esteem, or how something was a boost to our own self-esteem.

The struggle for self-esteem, however, can be likened to a game, a game in which "high self-esteem" is the name for winning and "low self-esteem" is the name for losing. Like any game, there are ways to win and ways to lose, and winning really doesn't matter; it only matters in the context and reasoning of the game. The struggle for self-esteem is a serious and popular game, but that doesn't make it any less of a game. We can continue to play this game if we choose, or we can stop thinking of our self-respect as dependent upon what we do, what we have, or what others think of us.

Dignity is the outward expression of self-respect. When we think in terms of grace, we can always live with dignity because our self-respect is always unconditional. We can live with dignity no matter what we have done; no matter what we have or don't have; no matter what our wealth, health, power or reputation; no matter what happens to us and no matter what anyone thinks of us. A woman can have a cancer that causes her to lose her job, her looks, her physical strength, and even her ability to clean herself, and yet still live with dignity. Personal dignity requires no justification. It is dependent upon unconditional self-respect alone.

Even if we are "disgraced" by our actions or circumstances, we can always choose grace; and in choosing grace we can always live with dignity. If we have done wrong, we can admit it and deal with the consequences while conducting ourselves with dignity. With grace, there is nothing and no one that can stop us from living with dignity.

Love

Love is another hard word to define, perhaps the hardest of all. Like *respect* and *forgiveness*, we have an intuitive sense of what it is, and of how incredibly important it is, but it is a hard word to define. *Love* sometimes seems to mean passion; romantic passion, as in, "I love you," or passion in general, as in "I love chocolate." But *love* seems to carry a larger sense than passion and may not even include any apparent emotion.

Jesus gives examples of love in the Good Samaritan and the father of the prodigal son. He also spoke of love as a choice, the essential choice that characterized his followers. He said: *A new commandment I give to you, that you love one another: just as I have loved you, you also are to love one another. By this all people will know that you are my disciples, if you have love for one another* (John 13:34-35). Love is often seen as motivated by emotion, beauty, nobility, strength, or sexuality, but Jesus spoke of it as a choice. He also raised it to a higher level than was common at the time, saying: *You have heard that it was said, 'You shall love your neighbor and hate your enemy.' But I say to you, love your enemies and pray for those who persecute you* (Matthew 5:43-44).

"Love is a choice." We may have heard that many times, and even agreed with it, but we may still struggle with the question of *how* we are to actually make that choice, especially if it feels hard, such as when we are thinking of someone who treats us badly. Jesus tells us how in the parable of the Good Samaritan. Although he told the parable as an example of love, and in answer to the question, "who is my neighbor?" the parable also provides an answer to the question: "How is love a choice?" The Good Samaritan is described as "having compassion." His generosity is also plain, as well as his respect for a man whom the priest and Levite evidently dismissed as unworthy of their time or attention. The picture we have is this: We act with love when we act with grace.

Love is a choice because grace is a choice. When, with grace, we make our generosity, compassion, forgiveness and respect unconditional, we think and act with love. This is how we can love both those who treat us well and those who treat us badly. This is how we can love those who are unlikely to return it. We choose love when we choose to think in terms of grace. We love one another when we think about one another with grace. We love our husband or wife when we think about them with grace; and we fail to love our husband or wife when we don't. We love our children when we think about them with grace. We love those with whom we work when we think about them with grace. And we love those who hate us when we think about them with grace.

We choose to love when our gifts are truly gifts. We choose to love when we act with compassion toward those who are suffering without considering whether or not they deserve it. We choose to love when our forgiveness is not dependent upon an apology. And we choose love when we regard people with respect, regardless of their behavior.

When we fail to think in terms of grace, everything is conditional: our gifts, our care for one another, our forgiveness, and our respect. Our love is conditional, given only to those who seem to deserve it. In the parable of the Good Samaritan, the priest and Levite acted as if their love was conditional. The Samaritan could have done the same; but unlike them, his love was not conditional and that choice led to an altogether different response.

There is no such thing as someone who is unlovable. Love is always a choice because grace is always a choice. We can love people even when they see themselves as more righteous than us; when their complicity hurts us; or they are stubbornly rigid in their self-justifying beliefs about us. We can love others even when they live in denial, or when they look down on us with their legalistic thinking. We can love others even when they gossip about us, try to control us, seem to hate us, or continually harass us. We can love those who add stress to our lives and drain our energy. We can even love others when they are hurting the people we care about most.

Someone may say, "Okay, but who can do that?" Grace is always a choice. In each and every moment, it is always a choice. Even when our emotions clamor against us, it is still a choice. And when we choose grace we choose love. Our love is unconditional, not because we are particularly strong or noble; but because our generosity, compassion, forgiveness and respect are unconditional. Our love is not dependent upon anyone's attitude or behavior. It is a gift of grace.

Loving God

When Jesus was asked about what he considered God's greatest commandment, he replied, *"You shall love the Lord your God with all your heart and with all your soul and with all your mind and with all your strength." The second is this: "You shall love your neighbor as yourself." There is no other commandment greater than these* (Mark 12:30-31). Jesus had been asked only about the most important commandment. But instead of stopping with the one, that we should love God, he went on to include the second commandment, as though it was inseparable from the first. For Jesus, the question of the greatest commandment apparently could not be fully answered without including the second commandment: *You shall love your neighbor as yourself.* Jesus shed light on his reason for doing this in a parable he told about a king who had assembled his subjects for judgment (Matthew 25:31-46). The king judges their attitude toward him by looking at how they have treated one another, saying, *Truly, I say to you, as you did it to one of the least of these my brothers, you did it to me* (v. 40). ... *And as you did not do it to one of the least of these, you did not do it to me* (v. 45). We love God to the same extent that we love one another, and we don't love God to the extent that we don't love one another. In practice, the first and second commandments are one. The apostle Paul reiterated this when he wrote, *for the whole Law is fulfilled in one word, in the statement, "you shall love your neighbor as yourself"* (Galatians 5:14).

Loving God is not just a matter of religious practice or devotional ritual; it is a matter of how we think about and treat one another. We love God to the same extent that we love all the people who come to our attention. We love God as much as we love our spouse. We love God as much as we love our children. We love God as much as we love our co-workers. We love God as much as we love all of the people we talk with in the course of our day. We love God as much as we love those who hate us and treat us badly. We love God as much as we love our neighbor; and we love both God and our neighbor when we think in terms of grace.

Love as a Choice

Love, as an expression of grace, is a choice that is independent of our emotions, our circumstances or the behavior of others. It is unconditional. When we think in terms of grace, however, our love is not merely unconditional as a principle; we are also *moved* to love. We have eyes to really see one another without the myopia of self-justification. We are not invested in seeing others as less righteous than ourselves. We are not blinded by denial, legalistic thinking or rigid conceptions of one another. Our perceptions are not colored by our complicit relationships or controlled by our overbearing authority figures. We don't look at one another with eyes of judgment. We look at one another with eyes of grace, eyes that allow us to really see one another. Our eyes are opened to see another human being with a human soul, and there is something about seeing a human soul that moves us to love. We are moved to regard one another with love, not just as a principle, but from our own soul.

Loving Ourselves

Just as we love others when we think in terms of grace, we love ourselves when we think in terms of grace. We love ourselves when we refrain from thinking about the gifts we are given as things we must deserve. And we love ourselves when we refrain from trying to judge whether or not we are worthy of compassion, forgiveness or respect.

Gumption

Gumption is a combination of initiative, boldness, common sense and determination. Grace frees us to live with gumption. It frees us to relate to one another with personal initiative and boldness. It frees us to look at our circumstances with common sense and determination. It frees us to take full responsibility for our lives, and make the very most of our lives.

The Good Samaritan is noted for his compassion, but he can also be noticed for his gumption. Like the priest and Levite, he might have just walked on by the man in the road; but he chose to stop. He wasn't told to stop, and he wasn't made to stop. He *chose* to stop. He took the initiative to stop and boldly take on a big challenge. And unlike the priest and Levite, he responded to the situation with common sense. Consider how self-justification can lead us to live with a lack of gumption:

- In abdication, we have a tendency to only do what other people want us to do. We have a tendency to only believe what other people want us to believe, think what other people tell us to think, and spend our time as other people want us to spend our time.

- Overbearing imposes a censorship, a censorship that may insist that we remain passive, stick to safe topics, or say nothing. We may only obey this censorship because we fear punishment, but we may also obey it out of a fear of losing the approval of an overbearing authority. Either way, we fail to live with initiative, boldness, common sense and determination. Rather than thinking for ourselves and speaking for ourselves, we allow our lives to be directed by someone else.

- Our desire for complicity with others can lead us to go along with their self-justifying schemes whether we agree with them or not. If we have different ideas, we may keep them to ourselves. We don't want to endanger our complicity by "rocking the boat." Our desire to be complicit with others can keep us from forming and developing our own thoughts, ideas, words, and goals. It can determine much of what we do, even to the point of determining our profession and the friendships we pursue.

- We may be held back by our legalism. Legalism leads us to be more concerned about breaking a certain set of rules rather than living with gumption.

- We may be held back by our denial. Denial keeps us from thinking about things. It keeps us from talking about things. It keeps us from asking important questions. And it keeps us from looking for needed answers. If we convince ourselves that everything is fine, then we may live with inertia rather than personal initiative.

- We may prefer to let others tell us what we should think and do, because then if something goes wrong we can assign the blame to them. We won't feel responsible; we can still feel righteous.

- We may hold ourselves back because we unduly value the opinions of others. We can fail to act with initiative, boldness or common sense because we fear disapproval.

- We may only give ourselves permission to act with gumption when we see ourselves as sufficiently righteous. Otherwise, we may not feel as though we have the right.

Some of us may say, "I've never had much gumption; that's just how I am. That's just how I've always been." But gumption isn't something that we simply have or don't have. Our lives may only lack gumption because we have lived with an investment in self-justification, and that investment has bound and constricted our lives in more ways than we realize.

Anemia is a medical condition in which our blood lacks the normal amount of red blood cells. People who suffer from anemia feel weak, tired, and lacking in vitality. As a result, the word *anemic* has been used to describe anything that is weak and lacking in substance or vitality. We can see this in such phrases as *an anemic effort* or *an anemic response*. We can likewise think of an anemic life, a weak life lacking gumption. Self-justification leads to an anemic life. Grace, as it leads us to let go of self-justification, leads us to live a life of real consequence.

Thinking in terms of grace can also allow us to see the ugliness of our self-justification. We can see the self-centeredness of our boasting, the cruelty of our judging, the blindness of our denial, the delusions of our rigidity, the self-righteousness of our legalism, the shallow camaraderie of our complicity, the oppressiveness of our overbearing, and the cowardice of our abdication. We can see the ugliness of it all and be moved to have nothing to do with it even if we must walk a difficult path. We are moved to live differently:

- We are moved to let go of denial and rigidity, and face the truth. We are moved to let go of our rationalization and sloth.

- We are moved to let go of complicity and legal-ism, even if it means that we must break away from particular relationships. We are moved to "rock the boat" if necessary. We are moved to develop our own goals. We would rather live against the grain of our society, risking persecution and even the hatred of others, rather than accept the illusory refuges of complicity or legalism.

- We are moved to face down our fears, such as our fear of an overbearing authority or our fear of being really known.

- We are moved to let go of our abdication. We are moved to think for ourselves and express our own thoughts.

- We are moved to set aside judging, unforgiveness and resentment.

The choice to think in terms of grace itself can also lead us to live with gumption. Grace isn't passive. It doesn't require us to be the proverbial doormat. It doesn't require us to be nice as others might define that word. It doesn't require us to live as others think we should live. We have our own compass: our thoughts, words, goals and actions are guided by our choice of grace over self-justification. Although we may still consider the opinions of others, we are not depen-dent upon their opinions. The Good Samaritan didn't need anyone to tell him to stop and help the man in the road. He lived by his own compass, a compass that led him to stop and help. He acted with gumption because he thought in terms of grace.

The choice of grace over self-justification also leads us to live with gumption for other reasons: We have a greater concern for *truth and justice*, we see *life as a gift*, we live with *fortitude*, and we *live with soul*.

Truth and Justice

Self-justification can blind us to injustice and falsehood. We may be very aware of when we are wronged, but fail to notice that there is even an issue if it doesn't affect our feeling of righteousness. And if we do happen to see that there is an issue, our strategies of self-justification obscure our vision: denial prevents us from seeing and considering important facts; complicity leads us to only think about things as our friends do; and our practice of holding rigid beliefs can lead us to fasten on to false beliefs. Self-justification may also lead us to simply play the Judge, think only in terms of the letter of the law, or wait to find out what our leaders think. When we think in terms of grace, on the other hand, we're not blinded or motivated by self-justification. We see more clearly. We are angered by the falsehood and injustice we see, and we are moved to act with gumption.

Inasmuch as we believe in the importance of grace over self-justification, we are also moved to stand for grace. We are moved to stand for universal respect and compassion. We are moved to stand against disrespect, unkindness and cruelty. We are moved to stand against the thinking that people should only get what they seem to deserve. We are moved to stand against denial. We are moved to stand against legalism and rigid thinking. We are moved to stand against overbearing. There are times when we are not able to take a particular stand, and there are times when we are wise to keep our distance from an issue, but our belief in the importance of grace over self-justification moves us to do what we can.

Grace is not passive. It doesn't require us to stand idly by while injustice and falsehood run free. When we choose to think in terms of grace we surrender self-justification, not truth and justice. Nor does humility require us to remain silent when we ourselves are unjustly accused of doing something wrong. There is nothing that prevents us from defending our actions in the name of truth and justice.

It is sometimes said, "You can only change yourself." There is much truth to that, but our lives can and do influence other lives (for good or for ill). Grace, as it leads us to stand for truth and justice, leads us to live with gumption as a person of consequence.

Life as a Gift

When we think in terms of grace, we see life as a gift; and to the extent that we accept that gift, we live with gumption. Consider the following analogy: If we give a bicycle to a child, and he takes to riding it like it has become a part of him, we know that our gift has been accepted. But if the bicycle gathers dust in a corner of the garage while junk piles up around it and the tires go flat, we feel that our gift has not been accepted. We can look at the gift of life in the same way. If we truly accept the gift, we make the most of it. Like a child with a new bicycle, we make the most of life and ride it for all it's worth. Seeing and accepting life as a gift leads us to live with gumption.

It's hard to ignore the sight of someone who is truly making the most of life. Such a life stands out. It is life as it was meant to be lived, as we would all like to live. We are all meant to live with gumption, and we feel it. When we see life as a gift, we are led to live such a life.

Living with Fortitude

The choice of grace over self-justification frees us from the heavy weight, false promises, and crippling consequences of self-justification. It frees us from a dispirited life with little meaning, and offers a real life with real meaning. It heals our relationships, and changes them into relationships that strengthen and encourage us. And most of all, it frees us to find God; a God of love and compassion, of power, hope, wisdom and truth, who, despite whatever may seem to be happening around us, is always with us. We may prefer to give up when confronted with hardship, but when we think in terms of grace, we can find strength to persevere and move forward with determination and even boldness.

Living with Soul

The choice of grace over self-justification also leads us to live with humility, and humility reveals our soul. We live as a real person, not someone who is merely pretending or playing a role. Our soul isn't hidden by our hypocrisy, complicity or abdication. We live truly. There is nothing in this world that stands out more, that is more interesting, and that brings beauty to life like the human soul. Self-justification hides our soul; grace reveals it.

In a world where people judge one another and imagine themselves more righteous than one another, where humility is dismissed, where denial is a way of life, where generosity incurs an obligation, where forgiveness must be earned, and where love is considered not much more than a feeling; we live with soul when we live with grace.

Gumption as a Choice

Grace is always a choice, and when we live with grace, we live with gumption; we live fully, with initiative, boldness, common sense, and a determination to make the most of our lives. Grace moves us to live with gumption regardless of who we are, regardless of what people think of us, and regardless of what we have done. With grace, we are free to live a life that matters.

Spirituality

Spirituality is a choice; a choice we make in the choice of grace over self-justification. We live with spirituality when we live with grace; and we don't live with spirituality when we live in pursuit of self-justification. We can see the truth of this in people who are widely recognized as spiritual. Their lives are not characterized by boasting, denial, complicity or over-bearing; they are characterized by the generosity, compassion and forgiveness of grace. Grace itself typifies spirituality.

Spirituality is also a transcendent quality; it transcends this world; it stands apart from and above all else. The same is true of grace. Grace is a transcendent choice that is inde-pendent of all else that is going on in our lives. It stands apart, and those who live with grace stand apart.

A paradigm shift is a fundamental change in thinking that changes our understanding and perception. We don't just change our thinking about a problem; we change the basic thoughts upon which all of our other thoughts are based; we see with different eyes. The choice of grace over self-justification creates a paradigm shift. In choosing to think in terms of grace, we don't merely change certain beliefs. We don't just change some of our values or make some changes in our lifestyle, however significant they may be. We change our whole way of thinking about life.

Faith

We live with faith in the grace of God when we let go of self-justification and live with grace ourselves. Consider the analogy of a house fire. If we believe that our home is on fire, we act like it is on fire. We stop what we are doing, alert the other people in the house, call the fire department, and so on. We wouldn't just sit in our chair reading a book or watching television. We wouldn't just say, "Yes, I believe that my home is on fire," and then just sit there. Likewise, when we believe in the grace of God our thoughts and actions are guided accordingly. We let go of self-justification and live with grace ourselves. The apostle James put it this way: *Show me your faith apart from your works, and I will show you my faith by my works* (James 2:18). When we believe in the grace of God, we act like it: we let go of our strategies of self-justification and think in terms of grace.

If it is our desire to live with faith in the grace of God, an understanding of self-justification can help us to see the meaning of that faith in some very real and practical terms. We practice our faith when:

- We stop taking refuge in denial, rigidity, legalism or complicity. We stop hiding behind judging, gossiping, or abdication. Rather than trying to justify ourselves, we look to the grace of God.

- We stop playing the game of who is more righteous than whom. We make our respect, compassion, forgiveness and love unconditional.

- We refrain from retaliation when others judge us, gossip about us, or see themselves as superior to us and therefore more righteous than us. We instead respond by choosing thoughts, words, and actions that are characterized by compassion.

- We love "the unlovable." If we find ourselves having trouble regarding someone with love, it may be helpful to consider how our self-justification is getting in the way: our resentment, our denial, our desire to look good, our desire to see ourselves as better than others...

- We live with generosity, and not only outwardly. We are generous with our thoughts of respect, our thoughts of compassion, and our thoughts of consideration for one another.

- We forgive those who have hurt us rather than holding onto our grievances.

- We allow ourselves to see, fully accept, and gratefully acknowledge the gift of life with gumption.

There are many things we may do in the pursuit of spirituality or a life well lived, but unless we choose grace over self-justification, all else we do may amount to not much more than going through the motions.

Righteousness

Self-justification doesn't lead to righteousness; it leads to *self*-righteousness. We may hate self-righteousness, and agree with others who hold it in contempt, but to the extent that we pursue self-justification, that is actually our objective, *self*-righteousness. We want to see ourselves as righteous, and we may very much want others to see us as righteous. We may only associate self-righteousness with legalistic religious fanatics or hypocritical politicians. But to the extent that we succeed in seeing ourselves as righteous, we too are self-righteous. Other people may not see our self-righteousness (especially those with whom we are complicit), and we may be entirely unaware of it ourselves, but to the extent that we pursue self-justification and think we are succeeding, we enjoy a feeling of self-righteousness and relate to others out of our self-righteousness.

Righteousness is important, but we don't find it in self-justification. We live righteously when we live with grace instead of self-justification. We live righteously when we stop pursuing self-justification and live with the respect, generosity, compassion, forgiveness, love and gumption of grace. When we look back on our lives and the mistakes we've made, we can often find that it was our pursuit of self-justification that was behind those mistakes. We made our mistakes because we were motivated by resentment, denial, complicity, self-justified anger, or abdication. We live righteously when we live with grace, and we fail to live righteously when we live in pursuit of self-justification.

Integrity

Self-justification leads us to be overly concerned about winning the approval of others. We want them to tell us that we are good. We want them to see us as worthy of their respect. As a result, we can compromise, sacrifice, or deny our personal values in pursuit of that approval. Rather than living with integrity, we abandon our values when they are not shared by those whose approval we seek. Inasmuch as this is the case, we live as creatures of our culture, thinking as others want us to think and doing what others want us to do.

Our self-justification can also lead us to live in ways that are inconsistent with the values we continue to affirm. Although we may value honesty, our denial or hypocritical boasting can lead us to live a lie. Although we may value truth, our rigid thinking can lead us to hold on to our own "truth." Although we may have a low opinion of gossip, our complicity with others can lead us to participate in it. Although we may believe in friendship, our abdication can lead us to neglect our friends. Although we may believe that everyone should be treated with respect, our belief that respect must be earned can lead us to be disrespectful. Although we may believe in the virtue of forgiveness and even encourage others to forgive, we may be unforgiving if we don't think it is deserved.

When we think in terms of grace, on the other hand, we live in accordance with our values. We don't have the same need for other people's approval. And we have no use for any strategies of self-justification. We also know where we stand because we have our own compass in life: We live in God's grace, and according to the values of grace. We may consider the opinions of others, but we're not dependent on their opinions. Our lives, and the values by which we live our lives, are guided by grace.

Prayer

There are two kinds of prayer: there is the prayer of faith and the prayer of self-justification. Jesus gave us an example of the latter in his parable of the Tax collector and the Pharisee. The Pharisee in the parable was praying, and his prayer was an attempt to justify himself before God. He said: *God, I thank you that I am not like other men, extortioners, unjust, adulterers, or even like this tax collector. I fast twice a week; I give tithes of all that I get.* Our own self-justification may not be as obvious in our own prayers, but we can do the same sort of thing. We can use our prayers to make a case for our righteousness; and if we are praying aloud and know that other people can hear us, our prayers may not only be an attempt to make our case before God, they may be an attempt to make our case to those who are listening. The prayer of faith not only refrains from self-justification, it is a deliberate renunciation of self-justification. In the prayer of faith, we choose grace. If our thoughts stray to self-justification, we direct them back to grace.

- In the prayer of faith, we choose humility over hypocrisy. In hypocrisy, we play a part. We wear a mask. We pretend to be someone we are not. When we pray with hypocrisy, we do the same; we play a part; we don't come before God with our true face, and we don't pray to God with our real voice. Such prayer is pointless; it may help us feel better about ourselves, but we are doing little else. Our prayers are not much more than an exercise in self-justification. When we pray with faith, on the other hand, we reject hypocrisy. We drop our mask and our (vain) effort to prevent God from seeing us as we are. Just as grace gives us eyes to see and ears to hear, it gives us a face to be seen and a voice that can be heard.

- In the prayer of faith, we choose love over judging. If it is our normal practice to play the Judge, we can carry that practice into our prayers. Like the Pharisee, we can use our prayers to point out the unrighteousness we see in others so that we can feel better about ourselves in comparison. We may even use our prayers as an attempt to gossip with God about other people's faults. (And if we are praying aloud, our prayers may include an attempt to gossip with those who are listening.) The prayer of faith, on the other hand, is characterized by the love, compassion and forgiveness of grace.

- In the prayer of faith, we choose generosity over selfishness. In self-justification, our focus is on ourselves. Our prayers are focused on our own needs, including our need for divine assistance in the advancement of our self-justifying goals. If we think of others, we may only be focused on what they seem to deserve. The prayer of faith, on the other hand, is characterized by generosity. We ask God to give others the same blessings we want for ourselves without thinking about what they seem to deserve.

- In the prayer of faith, we let go of the competition over who is more righteous than whom. If we try to see ourselves as more righteous than others, we may carry this into our prayers. Our prayers for other people can be judgmental, patronizing, or colored by a belief in our own superiority. They may also lack sincerity because if we are in a competition with those for whom we are praying, we may not really want God to help them. If we see that we are playing this game, we can instead pray that, after all is said and done, the people for whom we are praying will be found more generous than ourselves, more loving, more compassionate, more forgiving, more thoughtful, more thankful, wiser and even more righteous than ourselves.

- In the prayer of faith, our prayers are characterized by gratitude. In self-justification, we try to see ourselves as a person of worth, a person deserving of good things. Our prayers, therefore, can be characterized by the same attitude; we can come before God with a spirit of entitlement. In the prayer of faith, on the other hand, we think in terms of grace. We are grateful for God's grace, grateful for the graces of others, and grateful for all the gifts of life that come our way. In the prayer of faith, we pray with gratitude.

The prayer of faith, at its most basic and at the very least, is a deliberate exercise in choosing grace over self-justification. If we want to know God and really talk to God, we only do so when we choose grace. A life of grace and a life of prayer go hand-in-hand. Our best efforts to live with grace suffer without prayer, and our prayers suffer when we don't live with grace.

Spirituality as a Choice

The choice of grace over self-justification is a spiritual choice, a choice that transcends all else. We can choose grace regardless of our emotions, regardless of illness or fatigue, regardless of our circumstances, and regardless of whatever anyone else is doing. Grace is always a choice. We may not want to choose grace if we feel overwhelmed by emotion, but underneath that emotion, we always can. We may prefer to play the Judge, nurse our grievances against one another, and compete with one another over who is more righteous than whom. But grace is still a choice. Spirituality isn't merely something we have or don't have. We choose to live with spirituality as we choose grace over self-justification.

3

Healing with Grace

Come to me, all who labor and are heavy laden, and I will give you rest. Take my yoke upon you, and learn from me, for I am gentle and lowly in heart, and you will find rest for your souls. For my yoke is easy, and my burden is light. (The Gospel of Matthew, chapter 11, verses 28-30)

Self-justification is a heavy burden to bear, but grace offers relief from that burden. It invites us to let go of self-justification, and to the extent that we do, we can find a lot of healing in our lives. Self-justification not only causes a lot of pain, it does so in at least four ways:

Self-justification Hurts Relationships

Consider the effects of judging alone, which is one of the surest ways to hurt or even destroy a friendship. Consider the effects of other strategies of self-justification: Rigid thinking prevents us from really knowing one another. Denial fosters dishonesty in relationships. Overbearing leads to relationships characterized by stress, domination, dependency, conflict, and at times violence. Self-justification can do tremendous damage to relationships, relationships that have a profound effect on our emotional well-being.

Self-justification is Self-destructive

We are all familiar with how resentment can eat us up inside. And it's easy to see the self-destructiveness of denial. Our efforts of self-justification can also foster, maintain and worsen our feelings of guilt, anger, isolation, anxiety, stress and depression. They can lead us into an addiction, compel us to maintain an addiction, and leave us feeling helpless to overcome an addiction. Some have described mental illness as a dysfunctional reaction to a dysfunctional environment. We may similarly understand mental illness as a product of our struggle for self-justification in a self-justifying community.

Self-justification not only fosters emotional suffering, it can prevent us from maturing as a human being. We may grow older and more experienced; we may progress in social sophistication; we may advance in our professional field; but inasmuch as we are invested in self-justification, we don't really mature. We calcify over the years into our preferred patterns of self-justification.

Self-justification Hurts our Children

The effects of self-justification are far-reaching, affecting our children and our children's children. Our modeling can teach our children more than we intend, including our strategies of self-justification. Our children may then not only imitate our strategies, they may in turn model those same strategies for their own children. And so it may go from one generation to another. Consider any one of the strategies of self-justification such as denial, and how we can teach it to our children by our own example. Overbearing, rigidity, legalism, judging, and the competition over who is more righteous than whom, can all be passed down from one generation to another as a sort of family legacy.

Self-justification Keeps us Stuck

Self-justification not only creates a lot of problems, it can prevent us from truly addressing our problems. It can leave us feeling stuck, unable to find our way through our problems. Our denial, rigidity and complicity can blind us to the true nature of our problems. And even when we are able to see more clearly, we can still feel powerless to make the changes we need to make. It may even seem as though our ways of thinking and behaving are hardwired into our brains, and that we have no other choice than to live as we do. In a sense, they are hardwired. But they may not be hardwired into our brain; they may be hardwired into our ongoing self-justification project. When we live in pursuit of self-justification, we are invested in the thoughts and actions that support that pursuit. So if we try to change our ways, we are not just trying to change particular thoughts or behaviors; nor are we just trying to break habits; we are trying to change things that can affect our feeling of righteousness. If we make a change that hurts our feeling of righteousness, we are not motivated to maintain that change; to the contrary, we are inclined to resume our old ways of living, the ways that supported our feeling of righteousness.

Consider the example of gossip. If we see that we are participating in gossip, we may feel bad about it and try to stop it, but find ourselves caught up in it again and again. We may blame our failure on a lack of willpower, habit, peer pressure, or our upbringing; but gossip also supports self-justification. It can help us to feel better about ourselves as we complicitly join in with others to play the Judge. It can also be a way of distracting ourselves from things we don't want to think about. So while on the one hand, we may want to stop gossiping, on the other hand, we don't. Our attempts to stop gossiping can fail because it seems to provide self-justifying benefits that are too important to give up.

Our investment in self-justification compels us to think, say and do things that help us feel justified. Even simple and apparently minor changes in our behavior can seem impossible if they hurt our feeling of righteousness. We may give little or no thought to the concept of self-justification, and we may puzzle over why it is so hard to change. But to the extent that we are invested in self-justification, that investment can stop us from making the changes we need to make. Self-justification not only causes us a lot of pain, it can keep us stuck in that pain.

Grace as the Choice that Heals

Our choice between grace and self-justification can make a big difference in our lives. This chapter looks at how choosing grace can help our marriage, our family, and our sexuality. It looks at anger, and how our choice between grace and self-justification can make all the difference in how we, and those around us, experience our anger. It looks at guilt, stress, isolation, worry, addiction, and depression, and how grace can help us to find a better footing. Grace is healing, and it is always a choice.

Marriage and Family

Marriages flourish when they are characterized by grace, and languish when they are lacking in grace. Respect, generosity, compassion and forgiveness are essential to every marriage. Imagine a marriage that lacks any one of those qualities. Marriages lacking grace may have them in some form, but they must be earned; and if they are not believed to be earned, which can be often, they are withheld. Such marriages are also characterized by self-justification. They not only lack grace, they suffer from judging, denial, rigidity, legalism, complicity, overbearing, and the competition over who is more righteous than whom.

The same is true of a family. Although the term *dysfunctional family* is almost a cliché, some families are clearly less functional than others, and we can find a reason for this in a lack of grace. Imagine a family in which respect, generosity, compassion, forgiveness and love are lacking. Imagine a family in which there is hypocrisy, judging, legalism, complicity, denial, overbearing, or the continual orchestration of distracting activity. Families, like marriages, are healthiest when they are characterized by grace.

A Gracious Marriage

Grace is a choice and when two people choose grace, they can enjoy a gracious marriage. Such a marriage is not only characterized by grace, it is characterized by the love, trust, and harmony that are only found in a gracious marriage:

Love in marriage

In the parable of the Good Samaritan, Jesus portrayed love as unconditional respect, generosity and compassion. And at other times he talked about forgiveness, a gift of grace he illustrated in the parable of the Prodigal Son. When we think of these expressions of grace in a marriage, we can see how to love our husband or wife in some very specific ways.

It is common to think of respect and forgiveness as things that must be earned. And it's common to hear someone say, "He doesn't deserve my respect" or "She doesn't deserve forgiveness." We can think like that if we choose. We can choose how we want to think about love and respect and generosity and compassion and forgiveness. But there are consequences for how we choose to think, and this is especially true when we are thinking about our marriage. If we want to have a loving marriage, we are more likely to find that marriage when we think in terms of grace.

The choice of grace also leads to a loving marriage in other ways. In a gracious marriage, we don't fear being known as we are; we're not invested in only being seen as righteous, and our partner isn't invested in seeing us as less righteous than themselves. Nor are we invested in seeing our partner as less righteous than ourselves. We look at our partner with eyes of grace, eyes that allow us to really know our partner, see the soul in our partner, and love our partner from our own soul.

Marriages lacking grace, on the other hand, lack love. They lack respect, generosity, compassion and forgiveness; and love suffers accordingly. Love also suffers because couples don't know each other very well. They may think they do, but their eyes are clouded by self-justification. They look at each other with eyes of judgment; they're blinded by their denial, legalistic thinking, and rigid beliefs about each other; their perceptions are colored by their complicit friendships and overbearing authority figures. They may think they know each other, but they don't see one another as well as they think they do and what they do see is skewed in favor of self-justification.

Marriages lacking grace may appear stable at times, but the stability can be dependent on a mutual complicity between the marriage partners. Such marriages are bound together, not by love, but by a mutual agreement (usually unstated) to support one another's denial, uphold one another's boasts, reinforce one another's judging, and defend one another from the opinions of others. They are, in short, bound together by a mutual agreement to help one another feel righteous. Such marriages may appear strong as long as the marriage partners continue to maintain their complicity, but either spouse may at any time abandon the complicity and use other strategies of self-justification. They may, for instance, abandon the complicity because they would rather compete with their spouse over who is more righteous than whom; or they may abandon it in favor of other complicit relationships outside the marriage, relationships that may range anywhere from an intense affair to a casual gossip session with a friend. Complicity isn't fragile; it can stand against all sorts of assault and last a lifetime. But it can be quickly abandoned, and when it is, any apparent stability can be replaced by indifference or hostility.

Marriages may also be held together by overbearing. Imagine a couple in which the man is forceful about what he wants. He is overbearing, insisting on having things his way because that's what seems to promote and protect his feeling of righteousness. He censors conversation, controls his wife, and sets the emotional tone for the relationship. There may be an appearance of stability as long as his wife submits to his overbearing; but it comes at a great cost, and if his wife decides to resist, any appearance of stability can be quickly lost.

The stability of a gracious marriage, on the other hand, isn't dependent on complicity or overbearing. It is bound by love, the love that comes from choosing grace. And just as the choice of grace is a spiritual choice that transcends this world and stands apart from all else that is happening in our lives, so is our love.

Trust in marriage

Trust is earned, even in a marriage. It is not an unconditional gift of grace like respect, generosity, compassion and forgiveness. It must be earned. But we *can* earn it when we think in terms of grace.

Self-justification hurts trust in relationships. Denial, rigidity, complicity and overbearing all undermine trust. Playing the hypocrite and playing the Judge hurt trust. And if we are in a competition over who is more righteous than whom, we are not inclined to trust the person we are competing with; to the contrary, we are invested in seeing that person as worthy of little trust. Trust suffers whenever self-justification is present. The more we therefore let go of self-justification, the more we give trust a chance.

In a gracious marriage, there is no place for self-justification. Marriage partners think about each other with grace, speak to each other with grace, and generally relate to each other with grace. Trust is not only given a chance, it is encouraged to grow. Love, respect, generosity, compassion, forgiveness, honesty, integrity, gumption and soul, all invite trust. When they are consistently present in a marriage, trust can grow strong.

Trust, when combined with love, leads to intimacy; the kind of closeness that many of us dream of finding in a marriage. When two people relate to each other with grace, they not only find love; they find trust and intimacy.

Harmony in marriage

In a gracious marriage, we don't find the mere appearance of harmony that we see in a complicit or overbearing marriage. We find true harmony in which there is no competition over who is better, who is smarter, or who works harder. There is no keeping score. We enjoy the freedom to excel, explore, and grow as a person. We feel free to talk about our dreams, our struggles, and passions. We not only know that we are not alone in the world, we know that someone is standing with us.

A Gracious Family

Like a marriage, a family can be characterized by love, trust and harmony, but only when there is grace. When grace is lacking, family members don't really connect with one another and they can find it unwise to trust one another. And just as complicity may come and go in a marriage, it can do the same between the members of a family. At times, they may feel complicitly connected to one another; but at other times they compete with one another, attempt to sabotage one another, and find satisfaction in one another's failures. Consider some characteristics of the typical dysfunctional home:

- Personal respect is conditional, and when present often doesn't feel like respect. It may also be capricious or completely absent. There is confusion about who to trust.

- Generosity, when it appears to be present, has strings attached. Selfishness and materialism are more the rule.

- Compassion has strings attached, and insensitivity is more the rule. If compassion does appear to be present, it may be dependent upon complicity.

- Forgiveness must be earned, requires an apology, and is often a strategy in the competition over who is more righteous than whom.

- Love may only be a memory, if that.

Like the marriages that typically head them, dysfunctional families can be characterized by control, dependency, stagnation, anger, and an enduring sense of isolation in their individual members. They are literal breeding grounds for all sorts of addiction; and family members can find themselves plagued by persistent feelings of guilt, self-pity, rage, bitterness and anxiety. Such homes can also foster interpersonal conflict that reaches far outside the home.

Families, like marriages, are most functional when respect and everyday compassion are unconditional, not just at times or just for some, but for every family member, including children and those who may be acting badly. Generosity is a part of the normal fabric of these homes, and although family members may still be angry with one another, their forgiveness doesn't need to be earned. There is also freedom in these homes, freedom to explore, freedom to excel, freedom to express thoughts and feelings, and freedom from pressure to participate in gossip and other forms of complicity. And unlike dysfunctional families, they enjoy the kind of trust and closeness that is only found where love is unconditional.

Healing Marriages & Families

The personal dynamics in a troubled marriage or family can be complex: the various strategies of self-justification can change from moment to moment; complicit alliances can shift; emotions can wax and wane. It may seem impossible to sort out. But we may not need to sort it out. Troubled marriages can find healing as grace replaces self-justification.

And troubled families can find healing as family members let go of self-justification and start thinking in terms of grace.

There is no such thing as a perfect marriage or family, but grace is always a choice; and when people make that choice, they can find real healing. A gracious marriage is always a choice, and a gracious family is always a choice, because grace is always a choice.

Sexuality

Asceticism is an ancient and long-standing religious tradition that is based on the belief that we may become holier by practicing self-denial, austerity and abstinence, especially in regard to our sexuality. (In this context, abstinence is not just about abstaining from premarital sex; it is about abstaining from sex entirely, throughout our lives.) Adherents of asceticism withdraw from the world as much as possible because they believe it has been corrupted, and direct their focus to heavenly things. But inasmuch as God's grace changes our heart and shows us a new way to live, asceticism can be a denial of that grace, a needless capitulation to the corruption of God's created order. When we live with faith in the grace of God, we can reclaim God's created order for our lives, including our sexuality.

Although many of us don't adhere to asceticism as a general rule, we may still regard sexuality in a similar way. Much of the sexuality that is applauded and encouraged in society is corrupted. Many feel the shame of participating in such sexuality, and many have been hurt by it, often deeply. As a result, many have concluded that sexuality is best dismissed altogether. It may even seem strange to include the topic of sexuality in a book about grace. But grace can redeem sexuality and show us our way. Through grace, we can see our sexuality as a gift from God. We can acknowledge that gift with gratitude, and make the most of that gift with gumption.

A Sexuality of Grace

When we think in terms of grace, we can see our sexuality as an incomparable opportunity to know, and be known by, another person. In the biblical book of Genesis, it is written that *Adam knew Eve his wife, and she conceived...* (Chapter 4, verse 1). This use of the word *knew* in some translations has been derided as a euphemism, a puritanical attempt to avoid using the word *sex*. But there is much to this idea of knowing another person in sexual union. In sexual union, we can know another person in a way that we know no one else. We can know many people in an ordinary sense, but in sexual union, we can know, and be known by, another person in an extraordinary sense. This focus on knowing and being known can be understood as central to sexuality as God created it. When we lose sight of that focus, our sexuality can go badly and painfully awry. It is easy to see how the choice between grace and self-justification can therefore make a decisive difference in the character of our sexuality.

In addition to the focus on knowing and being known, the sexuality of grace is characterized by grace. It is characterized by respect, generosity, compassion, humility, authenticity, and integrity; all of which enhance trust, a trust that can allow an intimacy that is unknown to relationships that lack grace.

In the sexuality of self-justification, on the other hand, we not only want to avoid being known, our sexuality is colored by hypocrisy, boasting, judging, complicity, abdication, overbearing, rigidity, denial and legalism. Our generosity has strings attached. Our respect and compassion are conditional. Love may not even be in the picture. Self-justification makes sex ugly. Trust and intimacy are replaced by selfishness, greed, and at times, cruelty. The sexuality of self-justification also cheapens sex. Because we have lost sight of the focus on knowing and being known, we may only use our sexuality as a tool in the service of our self-justification: to boast, to gain acceptance, to get something, to assert our power or superiority, to restore complicity to a troubled relationship... This sort of sex may seem rewarding for a time, but it can also leave us feeling frustrated, used, and very much alone. If this is all we have ever known or understood sex to be, we may want little or nothing to do with it.

In this light, we can see that it is not sexuality itself that is bad; it is sexuality that lacks grace that is bad. Sexuality, when characterized by grace, can lead us to a deeper place than we find in any other relationship. When it is characterized by self-justification, on the other hand, it not only fails to lead us there; it leads to emptiness, addiction, or some other kind of pain. Grace makes all the difference.

Sexual Healing with Grace

Consider some of the ways in which grace can bring healing to troubled sexuality:

- Grace can characterize our specific thoughts about sex. We can choose to think gracious thoughts about our mate, thoughts that are unconditionally loving, respectful, generous, compassionate, and forgiving. And as grace replaces self-justification, we can let go of self-justifying thoughts.

- Grace can lead us to have sexual standards that are important such as fidelity, honesty and respectfulness; while allowing us to let go of needless legalistic rules that can inhibit our sexuality.

- Grace can characterize our beliefs about sex. Rigidity is a strategy of self-justification in which we are invested in certain beliefs because they help us feel righteous. When we think in terms of grace, we have no use for such beliefs, including rigid beliefs about sexuality. If we have thought of sex as naughty, dirty, bad, or shameful, we can let go of such beliefs. Those beliefs apply to the sexuality of self-justification, not to the sexuality of grace. We can choose different beliefs such as:

    "Sex, and my sexuality, is a gift from God."
    "Sex, as God created it, is not dirty or shameful."
    "My sexuality is an opportunity to deeply know and be deeply known by my mate."

We choose our beliefs, and in the sexuality of grace, we choose beliefs that lead to healthy sexuality. We can also adopt some intentional ways of being in our sexuality. If we have been passive, merely tolerant, or emotionally absent in our sexuality, grace can free us to be sexually present, express our sexuality with gumption, and discover the meaning of sexual passion:

Sexual Presence

When our thoughts are in the present moment, we are present. When our thoughts are elsewhere, we are in a real sense elsewhere. We are not present when we are worrying, thinking about other people, or thinking about other times and places. We are not present when our mind is far away. We are not living in the present; we are mentally and emotionally elsewhere.

When we are invested in self-justification, we avoid being truly present in our sexuality. We don't want someone looking closely into our eyes. We want to shut our eyes, turn out the lights. We don't want to be truly seen, by our mate or by ourselves. We are afraid of intimacy, of being truly known. When situations seem too intimate, we look for ways to escape, even if only in our own minds. Rather than truly relating to our partner, we joke, talk about unrelated things, and emotionally distance ourselves. We don't want to be known, so we "go away." We may seem to be present at times if we are caught up in a particular moment, but that presence can be as fleeting as a thought.

In the sexuality of grace, on the other hand, we can be fully present in our sexuality. Grace frees us from the fears and concerns of self-justification, and allows us to be right there, wholly in the moment. Just as grace gives us eyes to see and ears to hear, it allows us to be present.

Sexual Gumption

When we think in terms of grace, we can look at the expression of our sexuality as an exercise in faith. By faith in the grace of God, we can let go of the self-justification that afflicts us with the fear of being known. We can let go of the fear of knowing ourselves. We can refrain from seeking refuge in distraction or rationalization. We can refrain from trying to construct a self-protective fort with our overbearing. We can set aside defensive strategies of self-justification and stretch our faith in some intensely personal ways.

We can act with gumption in our sexuality, and take the initiative to face down needless fears. We can look at our fears with common sense and a determination to make the most of our lives. If we find that they're not valid, we can face them down with boldness and determination.

In the sexual gumption of grace we allow ourselves to be physically and emotionally known. We allow ourselves to be personally and emotionally touched by our mate. We allow ourselves to feel both our own and our partner's emotions. We stretch ourselves to be fully sexual with our mate, to live with grace as fully a man or fully a woman. And *stretch* is truly the word. In the sexual gumption of grace, we stretch ourselves in ways that we have not, and do not, in any other relationship. We make the most of our sexuality.

In the sexual gumption of grace we're not passive observers, dependent upon the initiative of our mate. Nor are we merely willing participants. We take the initiative to express our sexuality with love, boldness and determination.

Sexual Passion

Some of us lack sexual passion, and we may believe that this is just how we are. But that may not be the case at all. Consider the effect of self-justification on sexuality and how sexual passion may reawaken when self-justification is set aside. To put it another way, replace self-justification with grace, and the fear of being known with the courage to be known, and then see what happens.

Anger

Anger is our natural response to injustice, whether we are witnessing injustice toward others or experiencing it ourselves. Injustice is wrong and we feel it; and the feeling we feel is anger. We can all become angry at times. If we didn't become angry when experiencing injustice, we might rightly wonder about ourselves.

That being said, anger has a bad reputation; so much so that it is often seen as a bad emotion with angry people being seen as bad people. To an extent, the bad reputation is deserved. Anger can be ugly; it can be expressed with hostility, cruelty, disrespect and a spirit of malice; it can be accompanied by sarcasm, abusive language and violence. Many of us have suffered from other people's anger. And many of us have regretted our own anger.

There are two kinds of anger, however. There is the destructive kind, which has given anger its bad reputation. And there is gracious anger, in which, although we may still be furious or outraged, we think in terms of grace.

Gracious Anger

Although we may be most familiar with expressions of anger that are disrespectful and unkind, the expression of anger can be respectful and compassionate. We can be very angry, even beside ourselves with fury, while expressing ourselves with grace. It is one thing to feel angry, but even if we are furious when seeing or experiencing an injustice, our thoughts and words are still a choice and we can always choose to regard a situation or a person with grace. No matter how angry we are, we can think thoughts of grace and express ourselves with grace.

Anger is a feeling of determination, conviction, force, sincerity, strength, vitality, no nonsense, no shyness. We are prompted to take action, to speak up, to get out of our comfort zone and do what we need to do. We feel moved to address injustice. None of those things require us to be disrespectful or unkind. There is nothing about anger as an emotion that is necessarily cruel, inconsiderate or destructive.

With grace, respect is unconditional. Even if people act badly, we don't play the Judge. We don't set ourselves up as a Judge of who is worthy of respect and who is not. We may be outraged, but still regard others with unconditional respect. We can choose grace no matter how angry we are.

Destructive Anger

With self-justification, we *do* play the Judge. We give ourselves license to see others as less than respectable. We may even give ourselves license to see them as worthy only of our contempt or whatever they may suffer. Such judgments can then lead us to treat them accordingly, and our anger can be needlessly hurtful.

Self-justification also perverts the character of our anger, making it self-centered. We are not simply angered by injustice, we are angered by all that seems to threaten or hurt our feeling of righteousness, as if that too were an injustice. If, for instance, our efforts on a project are unjustly ignored while those of someone else are applauded, we may not only be angry because of the injustice, we may be angry because the slight is an insult to our belief in our personal goodness. We may be similarly angered by a challenge to our denial, legalism or rigid beliefs. Nothing, in fact, may make us angrier than an apparent assault on our feeling of personal righteousness. And we may fail to notice injustice altogether if it doesn't somehow affect our feeling of righteousness. If for instance we see an injustice to someone we don't know, we may be unmoved. But if a similar injustice is committed against someone with whom we are complicit, we may be outraged.

Destructive anger is often used as a tool of self-justification. We may use our anger to justify our words or behavior, saying something like, "I said it because I was angry." And we may use our anger to justify our overbearing, rigidity or legalism. Consider some of the many ways we may use anger to promote our self-justification:

- It can help us to feel big, powerful, righteous.

- It can assert our feeling of righteousness, and help us to feel that we are winning a competition over who is more righteous than whom.

- It can enforce our overbearing, and seem to give authority to whatever we have to say. If we want people to do something, our anger can be persuasive.

- It can reinforce our boasting, denial, rigidity or legalism; and intimidate others who may try to challenge our use of those strategies.

- It can push aside our feelings of guilt, grief or remorse; feelings that might otherwise hurt our feeling of righteousness.

- It can help change an uncomfortable topic of conversation, discourage others from challenging our ideas or behavior, put people on the defensive, and even silence them altogether.

We can also use anger as a tool of self-justification in what is often called *venting*. There are two kinds of venting. One is healthy and the other is an exercise in self-justification. In the healthy kind, we share our thoughts and feelings so we may feel less alone with our suffering. Such venting can also help us clarify our thoughts and work through our feelings. In the other kind of venting, we share our thoughts and feelings so that we can make our case; we try to justify ourselves, and hopefully find a complicit friend who will support our ways of thinking. We "need to vent" because we want to bolster our feeling of righteousness. We may say, "I just need to vent so that I can get my anger out," but we are actually looking for something different. And we may not be interested in getting our anger out at all; we may be more interested in stoking the flames. If we feel better after such venting, it may be due to the fact that it has helped us recover a sense of righteousness. Like all efforts of self-justification, however, venting may only help us feel better for a time; there may always be something that we need to "get out."

Controlling our Anger

Grace transforms destructive anger. Replace judgment with unconditional respect, compassion or forgiveness, and destructive anger is transformed at the root. If our anger seems out of control, we can take control by choosing grace over self-justification. Grace is always a choice, a choice that is always under our control; and in the choice of grace we can bring our anger under control. We can always choose grace, and that choice can transform our anger.

Grace also allows us to let go of our anger. With self-justification, we can be invested in our anger as part of a strategy of self-justification and have no desire to see it go; we can be motivated to dwell on thoughts that keep it burning, and look for people to help us stoke the flames. With grace, we don't have this investment in our anger. We may still be angered by injustice, but we can let our anger go as it is ready to go. Our emotions may take time to subside, but we have no investment in them.

Self-justification can make even the best anger management skills irrelevant. We may use those skills when it seems to be in our interest, but if we don't see people as deserving of our respect, or we want to put people down so that we can feel better than them, we may not. Some of us might find an anger management course useful. But even then, if we don't choose grace, we may not use the skills we learn. Many of us, when thinking of an ugly confrontation we had in the past, know that we could have acted differently if we had chosen. We act one way when we want to feel justified and we act another way when we choose grace. We may prefer to think of our anger as out of our control, but inasmuch as grace is a choice, as it always is, our anger is always in our control.

Constructive Anger

Anger, as the natural response to injustice, is not a bad emotion. It not only moves us to address injustice, it helps us to address it. Anger strengthens our resolve, increases our energy, sharpens our thoughts, and leads us to act with gumption. It can even override unhelpful and unnecessary feelings that may otherwise paralyze us such as stage fright. Imagine a man preparing to give a speech. He is paralyzed with fear at the thought of public speaking; but if he is angry about an injustice, his anger can override that fear. And if he expresses himself with grace, he can give an effective speech. Just as anger can be wrongly used to push aside appropriate feelings such as guilt or remorse, it can be used to push aside needless feelings such as stage fright. Anger can be used for good or for ill and we use it for the good when we choose grace.

If we are only familiar with destructive anger, we may see all anger as bad, feel guilty when we are angry, deny that we are angry, and fail to use our anger for the good it can do. But when we think in terms of grace, we can understand our anger, control our anger, and use our anger to address injustice without the baggage of self-justification.

Guilt

No one wants to feel guilty. Guilt is a troubling feeling that can leave us feeling weak, defensive, and at times desperate. It can leave us feeling detached from the world, detached from one another, and detached from life. It can leave us feeling dead inside, and make the world feel darker than it is. Guilt can also give rise to many other painful feelings such as fear, anger, hysteria, anxiety, depression and grief; feelings we may try to numb with alcohol, drugs, or as many distractions as we can conveniently or not so conveniently find.

We feel guilty when we believe we have done something wrong. We believe that we've done something we shouldn't have done, or failed to do something that we should've done. We can all feel guilty at times; it seems to be a normal part of life. With grace, we can work through it and do what we need to do to address it.

Needless Guilt

There are two kinds of guilt. There is appropriate guilt, which we can feel when we have truly done something wrong. And there is needless guilt, which we can feel when we think we have done something wrong but actually haven't. In either case, the feeling is the same. We feel guilty.

Needless guilt can be as painful and debilitating as appropriate guilt, but with needless guilt, we don't need to admit any fault or make amends. We only need to recognize that our guilt is needless. And when we truly see that our guilt is needless, there is nothing more required of us. We are free from guilt.

As might be expected, self-justification motivates us to see all of our guilt as needless, but it can ironically leave us thinking that our guilt is appropriate when it is in fact needless. Consider the following example:

A businessman has a heart attack. His friends rally around him and he shortly returns to work. But then he denies that he really had a heart attack. He fails to eat and exercise as he should, ignores the cautions of his doctor, and quickly picks up the same fast-paced, stressful life he had been living before the heart attack. He then has another heart attack which proves fatal, and his friends feel guilty because they think they should have done more to prevent the second heart attack. This guilt is needless because the heart attack was not their fault. The businessman was responsible for his own behavior. He was responsible for his denial. He was responsible for how he chose to live. The guilt, if it is to be assigned, belongs to him.

Like the friends of the businessman, we may likewise experience needless guilt if something goes wrong and we falsely believe that we are responsible. We aren't actually responsible, but for some reason we think we are. We may simply be mistaken about our responsibility, but self-justification can also lead us to think of ourselves as responsible when we are not. It can, for instance, make us want to think of ourselves as more powerful and influential than we actually are. Or it can make us want to think of ourselves as a caretaker for others when it is actually their responsibility to take care of themselves. Such beliefs can help us feel better about our righteousness. The downside, of course, is that when things go wrong we can feel guilty even though we are not to blame. We are not actually guilty because we are not responsible; but we think we are, so we feel guilty. Our self-justifying belief in our own importance can ironically work against our sense of self-justification by saddling us with needless guilt.

One of the most common reasons for needless guilt is related to abdication. If it is our practice to let an authority figure judge the rightness or wrongness of our behavior – as it typically is in abdication – then we may feel guilty whenever someone we see as an authority condemns our behavior. The authority may or may not be correct about our behavior, but our submission to that authority can still leave us feeling guilty whenever he or she condemns our behavior. Such guilt is not only needless if we have done nothing wrong, it is needless because abdication is needless.

We can also find needless guilt related to other strategies of self-justification. Consider the following:

- A man beats his wife. Afterward, he tells her that he doesn't like to beat her, but that she so infuriates him at times that she "makes" him beat her. She believes him because she is in denial about his true choices and doesn't want to believe that he doesn't love her. She then feels guilty for her role in the beatings and tries to make amends by being a better wife. This guilt is needless because she is actually not guilty for the beatings. And it is also needless because her denial is needless.

- Legalism leads us to fasten on to a particular set of rules that we hesitate to even question, some of which may be good rules, some bad. We don't see the bad rules as bad rules, though. We see all of our rules as good rules. And if we break one of our rules (even though it is a bad rule), we feel guilty, needlessly guilty if the rule we broke was a bad rule. We didn't actually do anything wrong. We only broke a bad rule. Since legalism has a tendency to give greater weight to the letter of the law over the spirit of a law, it can lead us to have a lot of bad rules, rules that if we break we feel guilty, needlessly guilty.

- If we think we must talk to a friend with whom we are complicit about something our friend doesn't want to hear, and our friend becomes upset, we may feel guilty. We have not only upset our friend, we have been disloyal to our complicity with that friend. This guilt is needless because we haven't actually done anything wrong. We may feel disloyal, but if our friend needed to hear what we had to say, we haven't actually been disloyal. We have only been disloyal to the complicity. Our guilt is also needless because complicity, as a strategy of self-justification, is needless. We may similarly feel (needlessly) guilty if we fail to support our complicit friend's denial, fail to support his or her attempts to play the Judge, or fail to support our complicit friends when they are criticized for doing something wrong.

Appropriate Guilt

Although a feeling of guilt can be needless, it may also be a signal that we need to admit that we have actually done something wrong. We need to admit what we have done and then do whatever we need to do to address our wrongdoing. That can be painful but doable when we think in terms of grace, but it can be unthinkable when we are invested in self-justification. If it is our goal to feel righteous, we don't want to admit that we have done anything wrong. We want to see ourselves as blameless.

Self-justification can not only keep us from acknowledging our guilt, it can blind us from seeing it altogether. And if in some situations our guilt can't be denied, it can keep us from doing what we need to do and even give added impetus to our efforts of self-justification:

- It can lead us to just go around and around in our thoughts, trying to find some way to justify ourselves or undo a reality that cannot be changed.

- It can lead us to blame others and find ways to see ourselves as better than others.

- It can lead us to rationalize about the circumstances that gave rise to our guilt as we try to make a case for how our actions were understandable given the circumstances.

- It can lead us to cling to denial and hold rigid beliefs that support how we want to see the circumstances that gave rise to our guilt.

- It can lead us to look for others who agree with us that we did nothing wrong, and try to see those who do think we did something wrong as doing so because they are biased, legalistic, ignorant, judgmental, or holding onto rigid beliefs of their own.

Rather than being motivated to do what we need to do, we are motivated to work all the harder to make a case for our personal righteousness.

There may be times when we think we have succeeded in escaping our guilt, but we never really do until we either see that it is needless or we do what we need to do about guilt that is not needless. We are better able to do both of those tasks when we choose grace over self-justification. If our guilt is needless, we are better able to see that as we let go of self-justification. And if it is appropriate, the choice of grace over self-justification can help us to see that too. If there is guilt in our life, our first step is to exercise our faith in the grace of God by letting go of the strategies of self-justification that are keeping it in place.

Self-forgiveness

As mentioned earlier, forgiveness includes the choice to refrain from playing the Judge when we have been hurt by others. It is wrong to play the Judge; in playing the Judge we assume a role that belongs to God alone. Playing the Judge, however, is not something that we may only do to others. We can also sit in judgment of ourselves.

We forgive ourselves when we refrain from sitting in judgment of our respectability. If we have been judging ourselves unworthy of respect, we stop. If we have been treating ourselves with disrespect, we stop. If we have been calling ourselves names, we stop. If we have been condemning ourselves, we stop. It is still important to honestly look at the rightness or wrongness of our behavior, but that is different from sitting in judgment of our respectability as a person.

Ironically, we may not want to forgive ourselves. We may not want to give up the lofty role of Judge. The assumption of that role can help us to feel righteous even if we are condemning ourselves. When we think in terms of grace, however, we have no reason to play the Judge; nor do we have any reason to puff up our sense of righteousness. We live in the light of God's grace.

Grace as the Key to Guilt

The grace we are shown by others can provide an invitation and an encouragement to let go of self-justification. In some cases, it may figure so prominently that we see it as the very thing we needed in order to find relief from our guilt. That grace can be a beautiful, life changing gift. But no matter how much grace we are shown by others, we don't find relief from guilt until we ourselves choose to let go of self-justification. The choice is ours. The grace of others is fertile ground, but fertile ground is not enough. We find relief from guilt as we let go of self-justification and think in terms of grace.

Stress

Emotional stress is a feeling of tension or pressure, a sense that things need to change and we are unsettled until they do. We can all feel stressed at times; it seems to be a normal part of life, but self-justification can make our lives more stressful than they need to be.

1. We can feel stressed whenever we don't feel adequately justified, and we can experience anything that threatens our feeling of righteousness as a source of stress.

2. Self-justification can worsen stress that is already present. Guilt, for instance, is normally stressful and we don't usually find relief from that stress until we have resolved our guilt; but self-justification, as it keeps us from dealing with guilt, prolongs our stress. And if we lie in an attempt to hide the reason for our guilt, we can feel more guilt and the stress associated with that guilt. Guilt is already stressful, but self-justification can make it worse.

3. Specific strategies of self-justification can add to our stress. Consider the stressful effect of rigid beliefs in a marriage (such as "He never helps."), or the stressful effect of denial in a work place ("Everything's fine!"). Playing the Judge can obviously make things stressful, and it isn't hard to imagine how overbearing can stress a family. Complicity can lead to stress when it causes us to compromise our values, and abdication can lead us to feel stressed if we think people don't like us. Although we may use strategies of self-justification in an attempt to escape the stress of not feeling righteous, those same strategies can add to our stress.

4. Self-justification can lead us to deliberately make our life stressful. As unpleasant as stress is, we may actually choose to make our life stressful as a strategy of self-justification. Consider the following:

- Stress can provide an effective distraction from things we find even more painful such as guilt or fear. And it can distract us from thoughts that threaten or hurt our sense of righteousness. If stressful events seem relentless in our lives, we may look forward to the day when we can finally find some peace. But if we value stress as a distraction, we don't actually want that peace. If things get too quiet, we may become aware of things we would prefer to avoid. So rather than being comfortable with peace, we look for ways to stir things up.

- We may value stress as evidence of how much we are able to endure. Just as someone might feel better about herself because of her ability to climb a mountain, we might feel better about ourselves because of our ability to endure stress. Our endurance may also invite the respect of others, which can also help us to feel better about ourselves. We may take pride in the stress of our lives, saying in so many words, "Look at all that I am able to endure. Look at how I have overcome such problems." Our stress can provide opportunities to hold ourselves high. We may therefore actually seek stress just as someone may seek a mountain to climb.

- We may see stress as a kind of punishment that balances the scales against our past wrongdoings, providing a sense of equilibrium to our lives. As a result, we may feel stressed, ironically, when our lives don't have enough stress. We may therefore look for ways to make our life more stressful just for this purpose.

- We may likewise value stress as a means of offsetting joy. In the thinking of self-justification, joy must be deserved. If we experience a feeling of joy but don't think of it as deserved, we can feel uncomfortable. An experience of stress, as it offsets our joy, can help relieve this discomfort.

- We can make things more stressful as a way of showing our power, with the implicit belief that power infers righteousness. The more we stir things up, the more powerful we feel; and the more powerful we feel, the more righteous we feel.

- We can make things more stressful in order to provide an excuse for our failures or as a reason for why we are not doing what we might otherwise be expected to do. A heavy load of stress can seem to justify a lot of things.

Much of the stress in our lives is needless because self-justification is needless. Take away self-justification and a lot of stress can go with it. Stress is a normal part of life, but there is much we can do to minimize our stress. Consider two other sources of stress, *isolation* and *worry*. In each case, we can see how self-justification leads to needless stress and how grace can relieve us from that stress.

Isolation

There are times when we all enjoy solitude, and some of us particularly enjoy our time alone; but no one wants to feel truly isolated in the sense of being alone in the world without any feeling of connection to others. It just seems to be how we're made. We're meant to live in connection with one another, and without a vital sense of connection we feel unsettled, stressed. Occasional times of isolation seem to be a normal part of life, but we weren't meant to live that way, and we feel it.

Self-justification can cause, prolong and worsen isolation. It can even lead us to feel isolated in the midst of people who are relating to us with grace. Consider some of the many ways that self-justification can lead to isolation:

- In hypocrisy, we pretend to be someone we're not, making ourselves unknowable to others. And if no one really knows us, we are alone, even in a crowd.

- We can isolate ourselves with our legalistic or rigid thinking.

- Our overbearing creates distance between ourselves and the people around us. Although we may feel in control of others, we don't feel connected to them. We feel alone.

- Imaginative boasting can take us into our own world, away from reality and real people.

- Complicity can offer an illusion of healthy connection, but it is only an illusion; an illusion that can also prevent us from finding real connection.

- Disrespect, greed and unforgiveness all lead to isolation.

- If we think of respect as something that must be earned and we don't feel like we've earned it, we can shyly hide ourselves from others and even push people away.

Self-justification can also worsen the normal pain of isolation. We may think of isolation as a judgment, as though we have been judged and found unworthy of the company of others. If we consider the judgment valid, we may not only feel isolated and judged, we may feel like losers in the game of life, sidelined, relegated to watching other people play, if we are even allowed to watch. We don't just feel alone, we feel like we deserve to be alone.

Grace, as it frees us from self-justification, frees us from the isolation it causes. It also delivers us from the faulty thinking that can make isolation more painful than it needs to be.

Worry

We are all familiar with worry. We can worry about the weather, about traffic, about paying our bills, and the well-being of our loved ones; we can worry about our office politics, the safety of our neighborhood, and the possibility of conflict around the world. There is no end to the things we can worry about. But just as self-justification can cause, prolong and worsen isolation, it can do the same with worry. If we find ourselves struggling with worry, we may find a reason in self-justification. Consider the following examples of how self-justification can foster and intensify worry:

- We may all worry at times about how we are judged by other people, but the more we are invested in trying to prove our righteousness to others the more we may worry. If, for instance, we are thinking about a recent conversation, we are more likely to worry about what we said, what was said to us, what others were thinking and what we should have said. We may worry about these things for other reasons but self-justification leads us to be overly concerned about what people think of us, needlessly intensifying our worries.

- We may similarly worry about what people think of us for something we did, something we weren't able to do; or about losing something, such as our job or health, that might make us look less than respectable or hurt our ability to prove ourselves a good person. Again, we may worry about these things for other reasons but self-justification can lead us to be overly concerned about what people think of us, needlessly intensifying our worries.

- We may worry about a possible misfortune, not merely because we fear the pain of the misfortune itself, but because we are worried about what the misfortune may lead others to think about us. Many see fortunate events as evidence of God's blessing and approval, and unfortunate events as evidence of God's displeasure. As a result, we may not only worry about misfortune itself, we may worry about what it seems to say about us as a person.

- In perfectionism, our standards are extremely high. This may be appropriate at times such as when we are looking over a letter for typographical errors. But perfectionism can also be an extreme form of legalism. In this type of perfectionism, we only feel righteous when we think we are doing things perfectly. This can leave us living on a knife's edge, always worried about making a mistake.

Isolation in combination with worry can lead us to feel especially stressed. Our worries may have no bounds and go far astray. They can color our whole world, setting aside more realistic thoughts. Self-justification, as it fosters both isolation and worry, can leave us feeling desperate.

Peace

Self-justification can bring a lot of stress into our lives, but the choice of grace can relieve us of that stress. Grace helps us minimize our stress, it helps us find our way out of needless isolation, and it delivers us from faulty thinking. It also allows us to find peace with God. If we don't think in terms of grace, we can feel alienated from God whenever we don't feel adequately righteous. Grace allows us to find peace with God no matter how unrighteous we may feel.

Addiction

Although we may normally think of addiction in connection with alcohol, drugs or smoking, it is also apparently possible to become addicted to other activities that may have little or nothing to do with the introduction of an external substance into our bodies. Gambling is an example. An addiction to gambling can share many of the characteristics of an addiction to alcohol or drugs, and seem just as binding. Other addictions may be focused on relationships, sex, shopping, viewing pornography, watching television, eating, working, cleaning, exercising, sports, or playing computer games.

There are a number of theories about why an activity can develop into an addiction. We can find one explanation in self-justification. Self-justification is a heavy burden to bear, and it is particularly heavy, painfully heavy, when we don't feel like we are succeeding with it. If we find an activity that seems to relieve us of that burden, or strengthen us to carry that burden, that activity can be attractive. We may not have thought of ourselves as burdened in such a way, and we may have never given a thought to the concept of self-justification. But if something such as alcohol seems to help with our burden of self-justification we can come to value it highly. If we have been struggling for a long time and find something that seems to help, we may even feel that we have found what we have always needed but could never find.

When we stop to consider the feelings we enjoy while indulging in an addiction, we can see how they can help relieve the burden of self-justification. Although we may feel shame after indulging in an addiction, we may experience a feeling of well-being at the time. That feeling may also be accompanied by a feeling of personal confidence, energy, strength or peace. It may even help us to feel like a person of value, someone worthy of respect. Such feelings can be compelling, and we may feel like we can never get enough of them. We may even be willing to sacrifice things we have greatly valued in order to get those feelings, including our friends, our family, our health, and our personal integrity.

Just as self-justification can dominate our lives, activities that seem to lighten the burden of self-justification can also come to dominate our lives. Even activities that were at one time benign can become addictive if we come to see them as essential to our sense of personal well-being.

This may be why we may give up a particular addiction only to replace it with another. The object of the addiction may not matter as much as the need it seems to fill. This may also help us to see why it is that one person develops an addiction while another person, doing the same thing to the same extent, does not. Consider two people, neither of whom is thinking in terms of grace. The one who feels less successful in self-justification is more likely to become dependent on something that seems to lighten the burden of self-justification. Although the focus of an addict may seem to be on a particular activity, the deeper focus is on self-justification.

The connection between addiction and self-justification can also be seen in other ways. It may be no coincidence that addiction is typically and even floridly accompanied by hypocrisy, complicity, judging, denial, rigidity, legalism, overbearing, boasting, and anger. Denial, in particular, is especially associated with addiction. Addictions begin with denial and are maintained with denial. And if there is a period of recovery, denial plays a part in a relapse. Complicity can also play a large part in an addiction.

We can also see a link between addiction and self-justification in people who are known as "dry drunks." A dry drunk is normally understood as someone who is no longer drinking alcohol but still thinking like an alcoholic and exhibiting the behaviors typical of an alcoholic. These can include boasting, judging, denial, rigidity, legalism, complicity, overbearing, and abdication; in other words, the thinking and behavior of self-justification. Addictive gambling and other types of addiction have their own version of the dry drunk, with similar characteristics.

If we find ourselves in the grip of an addiction, we may feel a lot of ambivalence about it. There may be times when we allow ourselves to see its destructive effect on our own lives and in the lives of those around us. And we may even see that what we are doing is morally wrong. At the same time, however, the addictive activity has become terribly important to us; we may not be able to imagine life without it. Such a thought may even be unthinkable. As a result, we may cycle back and forth between admitting that we have a problem and denying that our behavior is really any problem at all. At times, we allow ourselves to see the damage that is resulting from our behavior, and at other times we work hard not to see it.

Our progress in letting go of an addiction can go hand in hand with our progress in letting go of self-justification. The more we think in terms of grace, the less we need our high. And the more we choose grace over denial, hypocrisy, complicity, overbearing and rigid thinking, the more we can see the consequences of our behavior and the true nature of our high. Inasmuch as addiction is fostered by self-justification, we can find freedom through choosing grace.

Some of us may be able to walk away from an addiction without choosing grace; we may be able to find other ways to prop up our struggling sense of self-justification without the help of our addictive high. But as long as we fail to choose grace, we continue, like the dry drunk, to struggle in the same mud that led to and maintained our addiction. When we choose grace, on the other hand, we may not only walk away from an addiction, we may walk away from the conditions that fostered it.

We may look at the surrender of an addiction as an exercise in faith. By faith in the grace of God, we can let go of the burden of self-justification and our need for an addictive high. And by faith in the grace of God, we can live with grace ourselves.

Depression

Depression is a painful experience of personal depletion, degradation and diminishment; an experience that is often accompanied by feelings of guilt, fear, stress and fatigue. There can also be a loss of interest in food, sex, work and life itself. Depression has been described as a spiritual disease, a chemical imbalance, and a number of things in between.

Depression can be due to many factors, but self-justification can have a large part to play. Self-justification is ultimately empty and meaningless. It may provide a sense of meaning and a sense of purpose. It may even be what we live for: the hope of somehow proving ourselves. But despite all that self-justification may seem to offer, it is ultimately empty and meaningless; and if we come to see that without at the same time choosing grace, our lives can feel empty and meaningless.

A life of self-justification can feel haunted, or perhaps a better word is stalked, by a feeling of despair. If we stop and really look at our lives, we know that we are missing something crucial. It can seem as though we are living a lie or living on a stage. And even if others think we are doing well on that stage, we may wonder what we are doing on it.

Each of us has at one time or another wrestled with our purpose in life. We may wonder, "Why am I here? What am I living for? What is life all about?" Those questions often come to mind because we are living a life of self-justification and we feel the futility of it.

Depression is sometimes experienced as a deep and painful honesty. We may feel that we are being more honest than we have ever been before; and more honest than others who are only happy because they are not looking at their own lives as honestly as we are looking at ours. There may be some truth to that. Consider the following formula for depression.

Start with a normal life. Subtract some significant denial, rigidity and complicity (allowing greater honesty) but continue, and even add to, the self-justifying strategies of:

- Playing the Judge (which can lead us to condemn not only others but ourselves).

- Legalism (which can lead to further condemnation, as well as feelings of guilt and stress).

- Abdication (which can lead to repressed anger, a feeling of hopelessness, more guilt and more self-condemnation).

The result is depression, in which we feel the reality of our futile and deeply painful (self-justifying) life because we are no longer taking adequate refuge in denial, rigidity or complicity; but continuing to pursue our investment in self-justification. Self-justification can also contribute to depression in other ways:

- Our pursuit of self-justification can lead us to see evidence of our respectability in our job, health, beauty, skills, reputation, or material possessions. If we lose those things, we don't just feel the pain of the loss itself; we feel a loss of our respectability.

- Our pursuit of self-justification can leave us feeling isolated and alone, with little if any real personal connection with others.

- The consequences of self-justification can leave us feeling worn down. Consider the long-term impact of guilt, worry, isolation, and stress; and how self-justification can lead to, worsen and prolong those things. Consider the long-term consequences of holding onto grievances. Consider the long-term effect of a distant, conflicted or stagnant marriage.

Recovery

Grace contributes to both the prevention and healing of depression. Consider the following:

- Grace allows us to find real meaning and a real sense of purpose. It allows us to find a real life, a life we can live with our eyes open. It allows us to find a life in which we can stop pretending, a life in which we can really know and be known by others. The choice between grace and self-justification is a choice between two very different lives. Self-justification leads to an illusory, empty and futile life. Grace leads to a life of meaning, purpose, dignity, integrity, gumption and even joy.

- Grace leads us to stop thinking of self-respect as something that must be earned or deserved. It leads us to stop looking for evidence of our personal respectability; and if we suffer loss, we don't see it as a loss to our respectability. Our self-respect, like our respect for others, is unconditional.

- Our choice of grace over self-justification can help us find healing for our marriage. It can bring health to our family. It can help us find freedom from an addiction. It can help us find relief from guilt, worry, stress and isolation. It can change how we think and show us new ways of looking at our lives.

- Our choice of grace over self-justification can help us to find real personal connection, something we may deeply need. It can help us to find genuine friendships and a heartfelt knowledge that we are not alone.

We all need grace. We need the grace of God. We need gracious people around us. And we need to think and live with grace ourselves. We choose life when we choose grace.

Conclusion

A Culture of Grace

We use the word *culture* to describe the customs, values and beliefs that characterize a nation such as Lithuania, a geographical region such as New England, or a particular time in history such as the 1920s. We can also speak of the culture of a town, a particular age group, or a social movement. Individual businesses, churches, schools, and civic groups can each have their own culture. Wherever people gather together, they can form a distinctive culture.

Some cultures stand out because of their particular characteristics. We may think of a business that has a culture of innovation, or a government agency that has a culture of denial. Cultures may also stand out for their anger, fear, optimism, openness, negativity, prejudice, or grace. A culture of grace stands out for its grace and is characterized by the behaviors and thinking of grace. A culture of grace can offer some invaluable gifts. Consider three:

1. Although we may enjoy solitude at times, human beings were made for community. We were made to live in community with one another, and we suffer without community in probably more ways than we

even know. We may find a semblance of community in a culture in which grace is lacking; we may be surrounded by others who are interacting with us on a daily basis. But we can still feel very much alone. Where there is no grace, there is no real community; there is no authentic personal connection in which we really know, and are really known by, other people.

Where grace is lacking, we typically find the behaviors, thinking, and values of self-justification. Personal respect is conditional, disrespect is common, and trust suffers accordingly. Generosity and forgiveness have strings attached. We don't feel free to express our thoughts and feelings because they may threaten or offend the self-justification of others. We don't feel free to excel or take initiative because that might threaten someone's sense of superiority. Rather than finding community, we find complicity, overbearing, or isolation.

A culture of grace offers real community in which we can find love, respect, compassion, personal connection, and the freedom to grow and mature as human beings. And in a world that is otherwise dominated by self-justification, it offers a sanctuary in which we can find respite and perspective in the midst of that world.

2. None of us masters a life of grace by ourselves. We all struggle with life. We all wrestle with self-justification. We all have blind spots. We all lose our

focus and feel pulled back into our old familiar ways of self-justification, especially when we are still of necessity interacting daily with people who are invested in self-justification. In a culture of grace, we can find models of grace to guide us, encourage us, and give us hope. Grace is always a choice, and we can always choose grace regardless of what anyone else is doing, but we can find a lot of help in a culture of grace.

As an analogy, consider the challenge of learning a foreign language. Some of us may be able to learn a language by ourselves. But it can be far easier to learn a language in the company of others who are also learning it, and especially so if we are actually immersed in a culture that speaks the language. Such an experience may also help us to achieve a depth of fluency in the language that we might never achieve on our own. We can look at the life of grace in the same way. We can live with grace without the help of anyone else – it is always a choice – but we can do better when we have company. Though we must all walk our own path in life, none of us was meant to walk alone.

We also each have different aptitudes, gifts and talents; and many of us may not be as gifted as others in understanding self-justification. We are not all equally adept in non-concrete conceptual thought. Some of us are more practical minded, learning best by example. Although books can be helpful, some of us learn best from on-the-job training. We can find that kind of experience in a culture of grace.

3. For many, grace may seem like not much more than a nice idea, sort of idealistic or mythical. A culture of grace can offer an actual experience of grace in which we discover what it is like to be truly forgiven and respected. We can experience love and generosity, not as exceptional things, but as part of the normal fabric of a community. We can experience what it is like to no longer feel alone. We can experience real compassion. We can experience what it is like to be free of complicity and overbearing. We can experience what it is like to talk with others about topics that are even controversial and actually have a constructive conversation. For those of us who think of grace as the stuff of fairy tales, a culture of grace can show us the reality of grace.

If we have been accustomed to living in a culture of self-justification, we're used to being judged. We're used to things having strings attached. We're used to hearing gossip, and perhaps participating in it. A culture of grace can provide an awakening and a new vision for living.

An Intentional Culture of Grace

There is no such thing as a perfect culture of grace; not in this world anyway. But the more we choose grace and associate with other people who do, the more we can form a culture of grace. Any kind of organization can be a culture of grace, even a notable culture of grace, whether it is a church, a business, a school, a social program, a support group, a club, or a family. But a church, when it is true to its calling, is an intentional culture of grace; it is essentially and deliberately a culture of grace, with a mission of living and proclaiming the grace of God. Its purpose as a church is to define grace, teach grace, model grace, talk about grace, and encourage the practice of grace in everyday life. A church, as an intentional culture of grace, is a gathering of people who are consciously and purposefully choosing grace over self-justification. Churches may also, of course, be characterized by legalism, complicity, overbearing, abdication, judging, denial, rigidity, and the competition over who is more righteous than whom. But when a church is true to its calling, it is an intentional culture of grace.

Prior to the rise of professional psychology, churches were seen as the authority on personal relationships and a life well lived. Even with all of their shortcomings and despite the tragic examples to the contrary, churches have been among the foremost advocates of compassion, generosity, respect, love and forgiveness. Churches are sometimes dismissed as irrelevant to modern society, but a church, as an intentional culture of grace, offers a vital service, a service that is deeply and universally needed. Many elements of society now offer advice on living well, but no other organization has replaced the church in its calling as an intentional culture of grace.

Grace as an Agent of Change

Psychological counseling may be most helpful when it encourages grace, and helps people think and talk about the healing value of grace. Many existing approaches to psychological healing may be effective because they do just this: encourage or somehow point to grace, even if it is not called "grace." Inasmuch as the root of our pain is in self-justification, which can be the case more than we realize, we can find an answer in grace.

Grace is essential to counseling. Imagine a counselor who has little grace in either substance or style. Grace creates a safe place, encourages us to explore our difficulties, and allows us to honestly look at our lives. It helps us to see what we have been unable to see, and consider answers we may have been unwilling to consider.

A culture of grace, which we may find in any group of people living with grace, can offer additional advantages that are not found in traditional counseling. This may be especially true of an intentional culture of grace. Consider the following:

- If we only learn about grace in counseling, our experience is limited. An intentional culture of grace, on the other hand, not only teaches us about grace; it models, encourages and facilitates grace in actual community, a community in which a variety of personalities are each living with grace in their own unique way. In a culture of grace, we gain a real world experience of what it means to relate to one another with grace. We learn the meaning of love and forgiveness in actual community. We learn the meaning of unconditional respect and compassion in actual community. And we learn the meaning of gumption and spirituality in actual community.

- There are different kinds of health care including preventive, curative, and palliative health care. In preventive care, the aim is to prevent problems from arising before they start. In curative care, the aim is to cure problems that have arisen. In palliative care, the aim is to help people cope with problems that can't be cured. In formal counseling, the emphasis is typically on curative or palliative care. In an intentional culture of grace, the emphasis is on preventive care; and when problems do arise, there is the kind of help that is needed most: real personal connection and a supportive community characterized by grace.

- Formal counseling can take place in different modalities such as individual counseling, couples counseling, family counseling and group counseling. In an intentional culture of grace, the chief modality is community, in which many people gather together to support one another and focus on what it means to live with grace.

- Although formal counseling aims at providing a safe place to facilitate self-awareness and new ways of thinking, that place is typically confined to scheduled times at a particular location. Counseling relationships are also to some extent limited by the constraints of counseling and often end when counseling ends. In an intentional culture of grace, on the other hand, we can find safety in a gracious, flexible, ongoing community with numerous, natural, authentic relationships that can last a lifetime.

- In contrast to traditional counseling, in which a professional therapist is typically regarded as the vehicle of healing, an intentional culture of grace offers a community in which everyone may be a vehicle of healing; in their own lives, in their families, and in their communities.

- Apart from the authority of a counselor, some of the lessons learned in counseling may seem to have little basis. And as the memory of a counselor's authority fades, those who have met with that counselor may feel less motivated to live their lives according to the lessons learned. In an intentional culture of grace, lessons learned don't find their basis in a passing relationship. They find their basis in the grace of God. And in contrast to traditional counseling, which usually doesn't offer an over-arching worldview (or may offer one that is misleading), an intentional culture of grace offers a community-based worldview focused on the grace of God.

- Many who are suffering don't seek counseling. This includes people who have grown up in a troubled family; people who struggle with self-condemnation and feelings of guilt; people who feel lost and confused in a confused culture; people who languish in a conflicted, controlling or stagnant marriage; people who despair in their quiet moments. All of these people can find healing in a culture of grace.

A Culture of Healing

The world is full of hurting people. Those of us trying to help may find some satisfaction in our efforts, but we may also feel like we are just mowing down dandelions and failing to get at the real root of things. For many hurting people, the root of their problems is found in self-justification; it is found in the self-justification with which they live and in the culture of self-justification in which they live. Those people may find the most help in a culture of grace. When we can provide that, we are no longer just mowing down dandelions, we are offering a real answer that can make a real difference.

A culture of self-justification encourages complicity, gossip, denial, resentment, and needless competition. It perpetuates guilt, uncontrolled anger and troubled relationships. It fosters emotional immaturity, isolation, stress, addiction and depression. And most of all, it encourages self-justification itself, leading people to live lives of futility. We may be most effective in our desire to help when we provide a culture of grace, a culture that can provide a respite, a sanctuary, and a living example of how life can be lived differently.

Snapshot 1:

Strategies of Self-Justification

The following is a summary of the strategies of self-justification discussed in this book:

Boasting: of our worth, righteousness, attributes, accomplishments, superiority, possessions.

- Simple Boasting: "I'm a good person, and this is why..."
- Comparative Boasting: Seeing ourselves as more righteous than others. Playing the game of who is more righteous than whom. Playing the game of who is better than whom.
- Imaginative Boasting: Imagining ourselves as righteous.
- Hypocritical Boasting: Pretending to be more righteous than we are.

Playing the Judge: Trying to elevate our feeling of righteousness by focusing on the faults of others.

- Prejudice: Pre-judging others on the basis of some broad category such as race, sex, or age.

Denial: The refusal to see or consider something that might hurt our feeling of righteousness.

- Rationalization: Trying to construe things in such a way that we feel righteous.
- Self-distraction: Trying to distract our attention from things that might hurt our feeling of righteousness.
- Selective Insight: Selectively choosing how clearly and intelligently we think about an issue.
- Laziness: Idling our thoughts and shrinking our awareness to our immediate surroundings.
- Withdrawal: Removing ourselves from people or situations that may disturb our feeling of righteousness.
- We may also support our denial by: judging, boasting, blaming, threatening, joking, controlling conversation, seeing ourselves as a victim, spending time with people who support our denial and avoiding those who don't.

Rigidity: Stubbornly holding beliefs that help us feel righteous.

- Vehement rigidity: Adopting an intimidating posture in which we assert a supreme confidence in our beliefs, forbidding challenge.
- Withdrawn rigidity: Trying to keep our beliefs to ourselves. If they are challenged, we have no interest in considering the arguments.
- Hit-and-run rigidity: Asserting our beliefs, but then withdrawing if they are challenged.

Legalism: "I do this, this and this; therefore, I'm righteous. If you don't, you're not righteous."

Complicity: Working together to help one another feel righteous.
- Gossip: Validating and encouraging one another as we play the Judge.
- Working together on a self-justifying project.
- Supporting one another's strategies of self-justification.
- Defending one another from those who see us as less than righteous.

Overbearing: Trying to make other people help us feel righteous.

Abdication: Trying to escape responsibility for how we are conducting our lives by letting someone else decide what we should believe, what we should value, what we should do for work, and how we should spend our time.

Snapshot 2:

Living with Grace

We choose grace over self-justification when:

- We think of gifts as truly gifts, gifts of grace that don't need to be earned or deserved. Our generosity is thoughtful but it has no strings attached.

- We think of compassion as a gift of grace; a gift we can extend not only to those who are suffering physically or emotionally, but also to those who are trying to find relief from their spiritual pain through self-justification.

- We think of forgiveness as a gift of grace; a gift that doesn't require us to forget, and doesn't require an apology.

- We think of respect as a kind of everyday grace, the common grace we can extend to one another as a general attitude. As such, it is unconditional, not a privilege that must be earned or deserved. We don't sit in judgment of one another's respectability, and we don't sit in judgment of our own. Our trust must still be earned, and we may or may not respect how someone is acting, but our respect for a person is unconditional.

- We think of love as a gift of grace; a gift of generosity, compassion, forgiveness and respect. We think of love as a choice, a choice we make in the choice to regard others with grace. We don't think of love as something that must be earned or deserved.

- We think of life as a gift of God's grace, a gift we can accept with gratitude and make the most of with gumption.

- We think of spirituality as a way of life, a life we choose as we choose grace over self-justification.

Appendix

Grace as the Key

Grace is key, if not *the* key, to psychological healing. And grace is always a choice, a spiritual choice that has nothing to do with what we deserve, what others think we deserve, or what we think they deserve. It is simply and always a choice. We may not feel like choosing grace; we might rather play the Judge, take refuge in denial, or try to prove ourselves better than others. But grace is always a choice.

When we are hurting, when our relationships are suffering, when we are feeling at our wits end, or when we just can't seem to change, grace can bring healing. The following is a brief summary of some of the many ways in which this happens:

1. When we think in terms of grace, we see ourselves and the people around us with different eyes. We think different thoughts. We have different goals and values. Life has new meaning. (If we were to stop right here, the therapeutic effect of grace would already be immense.)

2. Grace heals our relationships. When we think in terms of grace, we regard other people with love,

respect, generosity, compassion and forgiveness; without any of which a relationship suffers. We let go of hypocrisy, complicity, judging, rigidity, abdication, denial, overbearing, and the ubiquitous competition over who is more righteous than whom; all of which hurt relationships. Grace is essential to healthy relationships. And inasmuch as relationships can bring pain into our lives, grace can bring healing.

3. Grace encourages us to let go of our denial, rigid thinking, complicity, and dependence on overbearing; all of which can take a toll on our emotional well-being.

4. Strategies of self-justification such as denial, complicity, rigidity, legalism, and abdication, can prevent us from seeing ourselves and our relationships as we otherwise might. Grace, as it frees us from those strategies, enables us to see more clearly.

5. Grace frees us from the self-justification that prevents us from truly addressing our guilt. It allows us to control our anger. It helps us to minimize stress. It helps us find freedom from an addiction, and a way out of depression.

6. Grace encourages us to examine our strategies of self-justification; and the more we see them for what they are, the less we want to do with them.

7. Self-justification not only leaves us feeling isolated, it leads to actual isolation. And it not only alienates us from people, it alienates us from God. When we think in terms of grace, we can move from isolation to authentic personal connection, with one another and with God.

8. The culture in which we live may try to deceive us, manipulate us, lead us astray, and seduce us into embracing unhealthy values and beliefs by appealing to our self-justification. Grace helps us to walk our own path.

9. Specific thoughts of grace, such as thoughts of compassion and gratitude, can help us break away from a train of self-justifying thinking, and even change our overall orientation toward life.

10. When we live in pursuit of self-justification, we can feel compelled to think, say and do things that seem to support our self-justification. Even making simple changes can seem impossible if they hurt our feeling of righteousness. Inasmuch as this is the case, we can find freedom to change when we choose grace and let go of self-justification.

11. A culture of grace can guide us and give us hope. It can offer a sanctuary in the midst of a world that is otherwise dominated by self-justification. It can also encourage us to let go of self-justification.

12. A culture of grace may foster psychological healing simply through offering the opportunity for authentic personal connection alone. It can also offer the compassionate eyes of grace, which may be psychologically healing all by themselves.

13. A culture of grace demonstrates an alternative lifestyle to that which we find in a culture of self-justification. In a culture of grace, we can find that self-justification and its defenses are not needed.

14. Inasmuch as a culture of self-justification can leave us feeling confused and struggling, a culture of grace can offer direction and purpose.

15. If our problems are due to a lack of information, we may be more likely to ask for information, and really listen to it, in a culture of grace. And if we have just been feeling stuck, going around and around with our own thoughts, we may also be more likely to find opportunities to work out our thoughts in a culture of grace.

16. If we feel alone and want to be understood, we may be more likely to find understanding in a culture of grace.

17. We feel most ourselves and we know ourselves best in the company of those who relate to us with grace. Relationships that lack grace also lack respect. They

pressure us to live by the values of others and pretend to be someone we are not. They pressure us to hide our true thoughts and feelings even to the extent that, if asked, we may not know ourselves what we think or feel. We know ourselves best, and feel most free to be ourselves, in relationships characterized by grace.

18. If we were originally taught how to relate to others in a family characterized by complicity, overbearing, denial, or the competition over who is more righteous than whom, we can learn different ways of relating in a culture of grace.

19. The choice of grace over self-justification can change our internal motivations. Self-justification motivates us to hold beliefs about ourselves that help us feel righteous. It motivates us to hold beliefs about others that help us feel righteous; beliefs about our relationships that help us feel righteous; beliefs about our workplace, religion, and the world that help us feel righteous. It motivates us to hold beliefs about our grievances, our prejudices, and about right and wrong, that help us feel righteous. It motivates us to legalistically think of ourselves as a good person because we do certain things, and to condemn those who don't do those things. It motivates us to gossip and strengthen our complicity with others. It motivates us to use people for our own ends, or to abdicate to gain their approval. Self-justification

motivates us to boast and accumulate things to boast about. It motivates us to play the hypocrite, play the Judge, and compete with one another over who is more righteous than whom. It motivates us to distract ourselves and deny things that hurt our feeling of righteousness. It motivates us to worry, fan the flames of our anger, hold on to our grievances, cling to our addictions, make our lives more stressful than they need to be, and live an essentially meaningless life. Self-justification motivates us to think, speak and live in some very unhealthy ways.

The choice of grace not only frees us from self-justification, it frees us from the motivations of self-justification. It also gives us eyes to see the emptiness of self-justification, motivating us to continue choosing grace. Grace moves us to live with personal authenticity. It moves us to let go of the competition over who is more righteous than whom. It moves us to face the truth. It moves us to face down our needless fears. It moves us to think for ourselves and express our own thoughts. It also gives us eyes to see the human soul in one another, further motivating us to live with grace. We not only see the value of living in the light of God's grace, we are moved to live such a life.

Study Guide

Our first concern in life is not with what's happening "out there, in the world" or even in the lives of people we know. It is with how we are living our own lives and how we are responding to the grace of God.

Whether we are aware of it or not, we choose between grace and self-justification in each moment of our lives. The study of self-justification can help us to see that choice, and the study of grace, both God's grace and our grace, can help us to make that choice; a choice that can make all the difference for our marriage, our family, and our own emotional well-being.

Week 1:

Read 'Boasting' through 'Rigidity' in Chapter 1.

Read the parable of the Tax Collector and the Pharisee (Luke 18:9-14).

1. How does the Pharisee illustrate self-justification?

2. The Pharisee uses boasting as a strategy of self-justification. What forms of boasting does he use?

3. How might a Pharisee use other forms of boasting?

4. How might a Pharisee play the Judge?

5. How might a Pharisee use denial? What strategies of denial might he use?

6. How might a Pharisee use rigidity?

7. How might we use these strategies with our husband, wife, parents or children?

8. How might we use these strategies with our friends or people we simply observe?

Week 2:

Read 'Legalism' through 'Letting go of Self-justification' in Chapter 1.

Read the parable of the Tax Collector and the Pharisee (Luke 18:9-14).

1. How does the Pharisee use legalism as a strategy of self-justification?

2. How might a Pharisee use complicity with other Pharisees?

3. How might a Pharisee use overbearing and abdication?

4. How might we use these strategies with our husband, wife, parents or children?

5. How might we use these strategies with our friends or people we simply observe?

6. What are your thoughts about letting go of self-justification?

Week 3:

Read 'Generosity' and 'Compassion' in Chapter 2.

Read the parable of the Good Samaritan (Luke 10:25-37).

1. How does the Samaritan illustrate generosity? How is generosity a choice?

2. How does the Samaritan illustrate compassion? How is compassion a choice?

3. How can we do these things in our own life? With our husband or wife? With our co-workers? With our parents or children? What stops us?

Week 4:

Read 'Forgiveness' in Chapter 2.

Read the parable of the Prodigal Son (Luke 15:11-32).

1. Forgiveness has two components: the choice to refrain from using grievances in support of self-justification, and the choice to regard offenders with grace. How does the prodigal son's father illustrate these two aspects of forgiveness? Why might the prodigal son's father have withheld forgiveness instead? Why might we withhold forgiveness in our own lives?

2. How is forgiveness a choice?

3. If there is someone you have not yet forgiven, ask: What stops me? How might it help to let go of self-justification?

Week 5:

Read 'Respect' through 'Spirituality' in Chapter 2.

Read the parable of the Good Samaritan (Luke 10:25-37).

1. Jesus said: *A new commandment I give to you, that you love one another: just as I have loved you, you also are to love one another. By this all people will know that you are my disciples, if you have love for one another* (John 13:34-35). How does the Samaritan illustrate love? How is love a choice?

2. How does the Samaritan illustrate unconditional respect? How is respect a choice?

3. How does the Samaritan illustrate gumption? How is gumption a choice?

Week 6:
Read 'Marriage & Family' through 'Anger' in Chapter 3.
Read Matthew 11:28-30.

1. How is self-justification a heavy burden to bear? What is the yoke Jesus wants to replace it with?

2. How does self-justification burden a marriage? How does grace unburden a marriage?

3. How does self-justification burden a family? How does grace unburden a family?

4. How can anger be gracious?

Week 7:
Read 'Guilt' through 'Depression' in Chapter 3.
Read Matthew 11:28-30.

1. Tell a story from your own life in which you felt burdened by a guilt that was needless. How was the guilt connected to self-justification?

2. Tell a story from your own life in which you felt burdened by stress that was needless. How was the stress connected to self-justification?

3. If you have felt burdened by an addiction, how was it connected to self-justification?

4. How does living with grace help us to find meaning in life?

Week 8:

Read the 'Conclusion: A Culture of Grace'.

1. The night before his arrest, Jesus prayed for his disciples, saying: *I am no longer in the world, but they are in the world, and I am coming to you. Holy Father, keep them in your name, which you have given me, that they may be one, even as we are one* (John 17:11). How does the choice of grace over self-justification help us to be "one"?

2. How is your family a culture of grace? How can it be more of a culture of grace?

3. If you are discussing these questions in a group, how is your group an intentional culture of grace? How could it be more of an intentional culture of grace?

4. If you attend a church, how is it an intentional culture of grace? How can you help it to be more of an intentional culture of grace?

Follow up:

Do a book study looking at how a story's characters use strategies of self-justification, and how they might instead choose grace.

Made in the USA
Columbia, SC
04 August 2020

15611648R00100